Love As God Loves

Love As God Loves

BRINGING HEALING, JOY, STRENGTH, PURPOSE
AND FULFILLMENT TO RELATIONSHIPS

Ute Stalford

Contents

Acknowledgments

I AM THANKFUL FOR ALL the women with whom God has allowed me to interact and with whom I have shared His love and truth, thus learning and growing together with them. I so appreciate my husband, who is my faithful supporter and cheerleader. I am also thankful for my special friends and family members, who gave of their time reading or working through the drafts of this study, commenting, correcting, adding, and improving it. Most of all, I thank my Lord, Jesus Christ, for walking with me in love through my life, molding and enabling me in my interactions with my precious family members and others to become more like Him. I want to share with you what He taught me, and I know it will impact your life just as it did mine.

A Symbol of a Struggling Relationship

LOOK AT THIS BENCH AND think of it in the context of relationships. It is broken down, neglected, and ugly. It no longer serves a purpose. It is useless—a sad-looking place and an eyesore, failing to do what it is designed for. Is it possible that some of your relationships with God or people in your life are also broken, ugly, nonfunctional, or a sore place in your heart?

This book deals with struggling relationships, as well as with relationships that are seemingly OK, helping to make them better, more meaningful and satisfying. Before you continue reading, look at page 100.

What do you think? The difference between the benches serves as an illustration of the difference God's love and its manifold expressions make in our relationships. **Only to the degree that we receive and internalize the many facets and expressions of God's love for us can we, in turn, love others with a love that reflects God's heart. Therefore, learning to live and walk in these truths is absolutely life changing.**

CHAPTER 1

Love as God Loves

DEAR FRIEND, LET'S LOOK AT some heart issues together. Are you struggling in any of your relationships? Has disappointment brought hurt and distance? Have walls gone up, causing isolation and brokenness? Do you wish acceptance and forgiveness came more naturally? Are you searching for a better way to reach, connect with, or impact lives for now and eternity? Be encouraged! God points the way as He reaches toward us with a love that overwhelms and shapes our total being. These expressions of love for us serve as a foundation and model for our relationships with others. It is His Spirit that enables His children to do the seemingly impossible: love as He does. Begin the journey of feeling loved with God's sacrificial love, which is unlike any other. Let it warm and fill your heart and then flow out toward others with a life-changing power that never fails. Follow each step with hope and the expectation of impact and change in your own heart and in your interactions with others.

I. ENTER INTO THE DYNAMICS OF SUCCESSFUL RELATIONSHIPS

"Love you" is a casual closure to a conversation that often bears little meaning and even less commitment to another person. How different is our informal statement compared to the weighty expression of love shown by our Creator! **He so loved the world that he gave his Son to die for mankind, which had gone astray** (John 3:16). That includes all men, women, and children. With that He changed the history and destiny of humanity. How powerful is the promise that those who respond to Him in trust and faith receive eternal life and spend the rest of their days as God's children. What a generous offer, what a costly gift, and what a life-changing promise. All this in stark contrast to our casual words: "Love you!"

Jesus Christ must have had much more in mind when He commanded, "A new command I give you: love one another! As I have loved you, so you must love one another" (John 13:34). He is so sure of the impact of His kind of love that He promises that if we obey His commands and love one another, God will live in us, and His love will be made complete in us (1 John 2:5). He goes so far as to say that this kind of love transforms us into true followers of Christ and authenticates us as such (John 13:35). When this statement is taken literally and we compare it to the reality of our lives, does a sense of shame, guilt, and failure set in?

The apostle Paul urgently pleads with us to thirst for, grasp, and personally experience "how wide, how deep, how high, and how long God's love is, filling us to the measure of all the fullness of God" (Eph. 3:13–20). He gives detailed instructions of its manifold expressions to strive toward in our relationships: This love is patient and kind. He continues with convicting descriptions and a bold promise in 1 Corinthians 13: "Love is patient, love is kind. It does not envy, it does not boast, it is not proud. It is not rude, it is not self-seeking, it is not easily angered, keeps no record of wrongs. Love does not delight in evil but rejoices with the truth. **It always protects, always trusts, always hopes, always perseveres. Love never fails**" (1 Cor. 13:4–8).

Notice the words *always* and *never*. Has this been your experience? Pause for a moment and ask yourself why. "Love" seems to fail more than it succeeds in our society.

Sadly, our culture often equates love with "getting" and asking, "What is in it for me?" Many of God's children are tuned in to the surrounding culture rather than to God's heart. Because of our fallen nature, it is easier to live that way. Divorce rates and relationship struggles and breakdowns are as common in the Christian community as in the secular world. Have we forgotten that as His children we have a new heart and a new spirit? It is time to get back to biblical basics and look at the facets of God's love for us as a model for loving others. When we do this with the insight, wisdom, and empowerment of God's Spirit, we learn to love with an unfailing love.

So, dear friend, let us start at the beginning. How is your relationship with God? Maybe you are a seeker. Look at the foundation laid by the work and Word of God. Ponder again the symbolic meaning of the two benches, and be ready for radical changes in your relationships! God's love is expressed within a relationship. God initiated that relationship with us through the offering of His Son, Jesus Christ. "For God so loved the world that **he gave his one and only Son**" (John 3:16). This relationship is a gift to all who are open to receive it, coming from His heart of love, an expression of His grace: "For it is by grace you have been saved, through faith—and this not from yourselves, **it is the gift of God**—not by works, so that no one can boast" (Eph. 2:8–9).

It is by faith that we receive God's gift of salvation and become children of God (John 1:12). Faith involves trust. God is the object of our trust. We take Him at His word. In turn, we internalize what He says and act on it with trust and obedience.

The love of our Heavenly Father becomes the life-giving force for us, His children. Giving and receiving are two key aspects of every relationship. And remember, my friend, mature love sees what we give as the bigger aspect of love. God loved and God gave (John 3:16). Loving is living out the life of Jesus. Our actions should mirror God's unfailing love. This description summarizes the essence of godly love, *for* us and *through* us.

Love is giving others what they need most, when they deserve it least, at personal sacrifice. Our expressions of love toward others bear witness of God's indwelling presence in our hearts.

What is the promise connected with this statement (1 John 4:11–12)?

Remember: **Love is a choice of our will**. Powerful dynamics are at work when we choose loving actions and thoughts. They in turn produce loving feelings. Unfortunately, we tend to look for the feelings first. Can you see the challenge?

Read Psalm 139:1–18 to give you a sense of the closeness and intimacy of the loving relationship with our Heavenly Father. Which aspect of these verses touches you in a particular way?

Also look at Psalm 23 and let the Heavenly Shepherd flood your heart with His care. You are His beloved sheep. Bear in mind that the well-being of each individual sheep matters to Him. I love to read this psalm before going to sleep. It calms my heart.

> **Only to the degree that we have experienced and internalized God's love for us are we able to love others with that same godly love.**

My chosen baptism verse was Colossians 2:6: "So then, just as you have received Christ Jesus as Lord, continue to live in him, rooted and built up in him." My challenge was to walk moment by moment by the rhythm of *His* heartbeat, receiving and living out His grace, His truth, and His ways in my daily life. The reality is this: **We live out of our inner world**.

Stop for a moment and discuss together the implications of this quote: **"You will always reproduce the environment around you that you cultivate within you,"** (Vallotton and Johnson 2006, 25).

Just as the thermostat sets the temperature of a home, your heart, warmed and filled with God's love, sets the "temperature" of your relationships. God Himself needs to permeate our inner core, soul and spirit, with the essence of His being and His love. This is what Paul meant when he said, "In him we live and move and have our being...we are his offspring" (Acts 17:28). Certainly, he does not describe a casual relationship, but the kind we need with our Father God to be at our best in loving others. This love is an overflow of what is in our hearts. We cannot give what we don't have ourselves.

Three things are vital in order to love as God loves:

1. Know the God of the Bible, His character, and His heart, personally. Do not just know *about* Him! Ask yourself what has shaped your perception of God. How accurate and real are your perceptions of the love our God has for you? Have life experiences or false teachings distorted these truths and painted a nonbiblical picture of God's character? Make sure you know Him as your loving Heavenly Father who reaches out to you with forgiving love. **Our perception of God**

will determine the character and level of trust in our relationship with God.

2. Be open to the experience of all of the aspects of His love in your own life.
3. Draw on His Spirit within you so that loving others becomes an expression of the life of Jesus in you and of the heart of God.

All three steps are dependent on an intimate relationship with Him and a walk of trusting faith and obedience. Do you have that? If the answer is no, it is OK. Just be willing to enter the journey toward faith and be amazed at what God has in store for you. **Ultimately, our relationship with God will determine the character and quality of our relationships with others.** In the following chapters, we will look at different aspects of God's love for us and allow God to show us more of His heart. Each expression of love will then serve as a necessary foundation and model for our relationships with others. For each aspect or expression of love, ask the following questions: How does this aspect of love express itself in God's relationship with us? How does this same aspect of God's love express itself in our relationships with others?

Numerous interactive Bible-study sections will help you discover principles, foundational truths, and guidelines to follow and on which to act. Please take the time to note your answers in the extra space provided. This will help you grasp God's truth and allow it to form your thoughts and impact your actions. In doing so, we will learn to function optimally, according to God's design, and to achieve our God-given purpose. We gain insights into how our Creator wired us for successful living, blending this knowledge with biblical principles and life illustrations.

In the application section, examine the following:

1. How is my inner life affected as I internalize and walk according to these principles?
2. What are the steps I need to take in my relationships to live in and live out God's love more fully?
3. What does the abundant life that Christ promised look like in my relationships (John 10:10b)?

4. Each week I encourage you to take just one specific aspect of love that you have had difficulty with and incorporate it into your relationships.

Remember, information turns to transformation when we act on it.

Let's get started with our first principle, the "as" principle:

- "A new command I give you: Love one another. *As* I have loved you, so you must love one another" (John 13:34).
- "Love your neighbor *as* yourself" (Matt. 22:39b).
- "Do to others *as* you would have them do to you" (Luke 6:31), also known as the Golden Rule.

These are short guidelines for the various expressions of love for others from God's Word. The good news is that **God does not give us a command that He will not enable and empower us to obey.**

What difficulties arise in your own life when you try to follow these commands?

Ask God to help you see these struggles and assess them honestly. **Only what God reveals can be dealt with and healed. Only what you face honestly can be changed.** If you are willing, share your struggles with your group for mutual accountability and encouragement.

We communicate love in actions, attitudes, and words. Love is an expression of our whole being. For us to be effective and sincere, there must be harmony in what we think, feel, say, and do. Paul says in 1 Thessalonians 5:23, "May your whole spirit, soul, and body be kept blameless."

Where do you see your biggest failure or challenge in light of this verse?

Look back at the passage from 1 Corinthians 13. What are your greatest weaknesses and struggles? Are you ready now to leave the past behind, choosing to look forward and embarking on a journey with God toward learning to love as He does? He is more than willing to teach you, enable you, and walk with you!

Communicate your answer to Him in prayer. Commit to pray for each other in your groups of fellow sojourners of faith. **After all, you work toward a common goal: transformation, healing, joy, new strength, and God's purpose and fulfillment in your relationships.**

CHAPTER 2

Accept People as They are

§

Being and feeling accepted are two of our basic emotional needs. Acceptance by others and acceptance by ourselves are closely connected. We need to know that we are OK, that we belong. A lack of acceptance fosters continued criticism of self and others, as well as loneliness, uneasiness, and shyness in social situations. We live under the burden of not measuring up, continuously seeking affirmation, becoming people pleasers or anxiously attempting to prove ourselves. We encounter failure with apprehension and easily give in to resignation and isolation. How very precious is God's acceptance of us, just as we are, with no preconditions.

I. How Does Acceptance Look in God's Relationship with Us?

When we became children of God, were there any conditions or prerequisites? No. God's simple invitation is this: **Whosoever believes may come** (John 3:16). The amazing thing to me is that God not only sought me out when I was still a sinner (Rom. 5:10), but He also accepted me as I was. Even more, the Word of God tells me that He is *for* me.

> How did Paul state this idea in Romans 8:31? Please take time to write your answer in the space below.

God Himself initiated the relationship with us! Can you see His heart of accepting love reaching out to you? For God chose us and called us, loved us, and adopted us as His children. Personalize and express in your own words Ephesians 1:4–5.

What does Ephesians 2:10 tell us?

Is it not amazing? He calls us His workmanship and His masterpiece (2:10, NLT), created anew in Christ Jesus? How can He not accept the work of His own hands, His masterpiece? The question is this: Did God compromise His holiness? Can I, a sinner, become part of God's family? God answered this question through an amazing exchange. I call it "the great exchange."

Put 2 Corinthians 5:21 into your own words.

God exchanged my sinfulness for Christ's righteousness as an extreme expression of His love. The great exchange happened on the cross. Do you remember the definition of love? Love is giving others what they need most when they deserve it least, at personal cost. God's love for us came at a personal cost to Himself: the life of His Son, our Savior, Jesus Christ. His acceptance had nothing to do with who we are but with what Christ did and how God sees us as a result: clothed with the righteousness of Christ. That means that in our relationship with Christ we are made right with God because He paid the penalty of our sin on the cross. Wow! Scripture talks about His children, also called saints, wearing white robes of righteousness. This is a physical picture of heaven describing this spiritual reality here on earth. It becomes an important part of our new identity in Christ as a child of God. Pause for a moment to ponder and ask yourself how your old identity was formed! Upbringing, education, people of influence in your life, and your accomplishments all played a role. Identity struggles are very common and can lead us along a treacherous path in life.

Friend, rejoice! Do you see a whole new identity for yourself, given to you by your Heavenly Father? He says that He welcomes you because of the righteousness of Christ credited to your account. You are the called, accepted, adopted, beloved child of God! You have a completely new standing as a member of His family.

To summarize these truths, remember: **"You are no longer defined by what you have done wrong. You are defined by what Christ has**

done right. His righteousness is your identity. His righteousness is your destiny" (Mark Batterson, 2011, 140). How easy it was in the past to allow mistakes and failures to define us, or to allow other people to define who we are! Now, we stand clothed in the righteousness of Christ and our God-given identity! This is so important because we act out of our identity. When Paul talks in Ephesians 4:22–24 about taking off the old self and putting on the new self, he points to the practical working out of these truths in a redeemed child of God. **Choose to bring your actions, attitudes, feelings, and thoughts in line with who God says you are. Be amazed at the process of transformation!** In the following verses, read about the permanence of God's accepting love for you, His child.

Explain Romans 8:38–39, in your own words.

Does this passage not say that this acceptance and new status is "once and for all"? You have a very secure and permanent place in God's heart! He will never give up on you! What you do or don't do will never again define who you are. Now, rest in these truths and know that your new standing in His kingdom is eternal and that you have an eternal relationship with God. Stop for a moment to praise His goodness and faithfulness.

II. The Need for Self-Acceptance and Self-Love

Dear friend, do you recognize yourself? God has redefined you! Remember, He chose you. He accepted you. More than that, He adopted you into His family. You are a new creation in Christ Jesus. He, the Creator, calls you His workmanship, even His masterpiece. Wow. He refashioned you and clothed you with the righteousness of Christ. That is how he sees you. There is more of the "new you" in the coming chapters, just because He loves you.

Paul commented on the connection between God's acceptance and your self-acceptance. He states, "By the grace of God I am what I am and his grace to me was not without effect" (1 Cor. 15:10a). He acknowledged that God's accepting love had been at work in and through his own life, producing a healthy self-acceptance and fruitfulness in his ministry. He reminded us that if God is for us, who can be against us (Rom. 8:31)?

Unfortunately, a lack of self-acceptance often acts like a debilitating disease of our soul that grieves God's heart. Henri J. M. Nouwen, one of the greatest theological thinkers of our time, calls the lack of self-acceptance one of believers' greatest sins. Imagine this: You have just painted a masterpiece. It is exactly what you wanted. Instead of praise, it meets constant criticism. How does that make you feel? In this case, God is the painter and you are the critic. It breaks God's heart when you don't accept His validation of you, His masterpiece. Remember the psalmist's words: "I praise you because I am fearfully and wonderfully made; your works are wonderful. I know that full well" (Ps. 139:14).

In my early days as a child of God, I repeated Romans 8:31 and 2 Corinthians 5:21 over and over until these truths sank in, and I began to feel so deeply accepted by God that I stopped being "against myself." After all, the Holy Creator, God Himself, was for me. I tried to picture myself clothed with the white robe of His righteousness and the beauty of His heart. I became increasingly self-assured and freed from inhibitions and social judgments. All of us, as we grow deeper in experiencing God's unconditional love, grow in self-acceptance. We become comfortable, at ease and at rest with ourselves. In addition, some interesting dynamics in our relationships with others begin to develop. We become more self-assured and are more secure in our encounters with others. This sense of security fosters acceptance from others, disarms society's bullies, curtails harmful self-criticism, and helps us set boundaries.

Moreover, as we experience and own God's accepting love for us and grow in self-acceptance, we come to accept others more readily. A marriage counselor correctly stated that the most important relationship we will ever have is with ourselves. If we struggle with self-criticism and self-doubt, we become "high-maintenance people," have little to give to our partners, and tend to weigh the relationship down with our own needs and suspicions.

> **Matthew 22:39 shows us God's clear connection between loving ourselves and loving others. A healthy love and acceptance of self certainly facilitates loving others.**

What is God's command in Matthew 22:39?

> Discuss in your group why God has wired us this way. Give a picture of a soul that feels well loved. Do you think that feeling accepted meets a basic human need? Why does it become easier to focus outward if we accept ourselves?

Think about it! God knows us at our worst and yet, in love, **He accepts us as we are and gave us His best**—that is, His Son. He did this with the sole purpose of helping us become our best, to share His accepting love with others, and to spend all eternity with Him.

III. Accept Others as They Are

Accepting others as they are means loving them unconditionally. In Romans 15:7, God gives a clear command: "Accept one another, then, just as Christ accepted you, in order to bring praise to God" (Rom. 15:7). Remember, my friend, He has accepted you and me exactly as we are, including all our blemishes and a heap of sin against Him. Notice this: Accepting others as an expression of love does not mean we approve of or condone their practices or even agree with them. It means we love unconditionally, with our love focused on them, not their behavior. The individual is always more important than the issue we might find unacceptable. It is said, "Love the sinner but not the sin." As already noted, our deep sense of God's accepting love toward us and our resulting self-acceptance are the foundation of accepting others with that same kind of love.

> Christ showed accepting love toward all kinds of "unacceptable people." Among them were sinners, tax collectors, and prostitutes (Matt. 11:19). Read the story of Jesus with the woman at the well in John 4. How does Jesus interact with the woman?

By engaging with her in a lengthy conversation, He breaks all existing social, moral, and religious taboos. Do you see how Christ, while ultimately exposing her sin, shows acceptance of her as a person by asking her to meet His need and even honoring her by sharing deep spiritual truth? Do you see how His accepting love produces increasing levels of openness, trust, and honesty in the woman? He is thus able to tap into her deep spiritual thirst and make her the first evangelist.

Some of the people you struggle with might be among those whom God Himself has already accepted and even pronounced righteous. For surely God looks at all of us with that same accepting love. Who are we to deny acceptance to others?

How can we express acceptance of a person in daily life? First and most important, look at the ways demonstrated by Christ! Many people with gracious hearts serve as examples as well. I remember a dear friend, commenting on the possible philandering of her husband: "I accepted him with all the good and the bad." That just about says it. When you go shopping, you might buy things that are marked "purchase as is." Accepting others in God's way implies "loving them as is." In practice, that means that our interactions with others are based on who they are and where in life they stand, and not on who and where we would like them to be. Thus your acceptance when raising a wayward child is different than your acceptance when you are dealing with an elderly parent or a friend who is struggling emotionally. In all situations, understanding, tolerance, and plenty of grace and wisdom are required. **Satan would have us major in the blame-and-shame game instead.**

One of the hardest things to live with is shame. Some time ago, a twelve-year-old boy hanged himself. Why? The next day was his first day at a new school. He was overweight, and he dreaded being taunted by other children. His false shame was too painful to live with. The miserable boy feared rejection so much so that this fear brought him to despair. One of the greatest kindnesses we can show others is to help take away their false sense of shame through acceptance, encouraging love, and understanding. In so doing, we help them to walk toward change and to find honor and a sense of personal dignity.

Sadly, our human nature finds it easier to judge and label than to show accepting love. This attitude is called self-righteousness, and God finds it as grievous as unrighteousness. Often when we don't accept people as they are, we show a lack of understanding or patience and increased frustration and anger toward them. Then, they feel as if they are walking on eggshells or through a minefield. They are uneasy in our presence. Their free expression becomes hampered because they feel they never measure up to our expectations. They easily feel condemned and judged. In addition, failing to express accepting love toward others closes the door to effective communication, so we lose access to their hearts and are certainly prevented from helping them change or to share with them the good news of God's love.

What do you think as you look into God's Word? Is there a place for a judgmental, critical, demeaning, or self-righteous attitude? What warnings do Matthew 7:1 and Luke 6:37 give?

As you see, God points to our individual responsibility before Him, making room for allowable differences. Judgment belongs to him. Go to Romans 14:1–10 for a deeper understanding and note your answer.

How effectively Paul models acceptance and going the extra mile to reach people's hearts for Jesus! Read 1 Corinthians 9:19–23. Put the essence of those verses into your own words.

Paul knew that accepting love means entering into other people's lives and walking in their shoes. This experience gives us access to their thinking and inner being. As we share in their world and walk some distance together in love and understanding, we also gain access to their hearts and influence in their lives. Most important, we open the doorway through which we can bring God's truth and grace to them. **We are humbled to be used as God's tools to help bring salvation and transformation, giving us a unique purpose for our lives.**

IV. Principles at Work

1. Notice the "as principle." We are to accept others as Christ accepted us (Rom. 15:7). Does that seem too difficult? God never gives us a command without enabling us to carry it out. What do Philippians 2:13 and 4:13 promise to His children?
2. He will indeed empower us. I like to call this promise the **"empowerment principle."** Principles are truths from the Word of God to stand on and live by in our daily walk of faith, bringing us into greater dependence on Him. Empowerment is the Holy Spirit working in us to will and to do God's bidding.

What does Romans 8:26–27 promise you?

Also read 2 Thessalonians 5:23–24. What promise follows the command to be blameless in all aspects of our lives—body, soul, and spirit?

Is this promise hard to understand, dear friend? Here is how it works. When God calls and accepts us as His children, a mystical, spiritual union begins. When we become children of God, He deposits seeds of His Spirit into our dead spirit. We could say He gives us a new spiritual DNA. In this conversation with Nicodemus, Jesus calls salvation a "spiritual birth" (John 3:1–8). Our spirit, dead because of sin, comes to life with the infusion of God's Spirit into it. **It is His Spirit that becomes our power source, the great enabler.**

Read John 3:1–8. Which part is the most amazing to you?

In John 15: 1–14, this union is described as the vine and the branches. Summarize this passage in a few sentences in your own words. Who are you in this illustration? From where does the life energy of the branches come?

Look at Romans 5:10. His Spirit life becomes our spirit life and power source. For united with Him in spirit, we become one spirit (1

Cor. 6:17). Please record the amazing truths you glean from these scriptures.

We are equipped for life and ministry, dear brothers and sisters in Christ! Now it is up to us to make choices in our thought, life, attitudes, and actions congruent with the life the Spirit is bringing forth in us. Love is not a feeling. It is a choice, an action. It is drawing on God's love within us and bringing our actions and feelings into conformity with the characteristics of that supernatural love. **Yes, dear friend, it is possible to love and accept others as God does, because His very Spirit within us becomes the expression of that accepting love.**

V. APPLICATION

1. How is your inner life affected as you internalize and walk in the truth of God's love and acceptance of you? Do you feel loved, secure, cherished, and at peace?

2. How should God's unconditional and accepting love influence your prayer life? Think of a well-loved child who is troubled and needs to climb on his daddy's lap to unburden his heart and get help. Are you coming to your Heavenly Father with that same confidence?

3. How can you demonstrate accepting love toward another person? Share a success story from your own life to encourage someone else.

4. Choose one verse from this chapter of God's love and acceptance for you and memorize it. Meditate on it every day. Say it aloud as often as you can. Put it on a sticky note, fasten it to your bathroom mirror, and ponder it daily. Do the same with another verse addressing your accepting love for others. This activity "programs" these truths into your mind and makes them more real in your life and actions.

5. What practical steps do you need or plan to take to love and accept another individual with whom you currently have a conflict? Ask God to bring conviction and insight into your heart.

6. How has this study made a difference in your relationship with God or others? It is important that we share our journey and encourage each other to take decisive steps in loving as God loves.

CHAPTER 3
Believe in What People can Become

ONE OF THE GREATEST GIFTS we can receive is others' belief in us and even boasting of what we can become. This kind of support gives us hope, self-assurance, confidence through today, and high expectations for our future. These people are "the wind beneath our wings." No one models this better than our Heavenly Father!

I. HOW DOES GOD DEMONSTRATE BELIEVING AND BOASTING OF WHAT WE CAN BECOME?

You might have heard it said that God loves us enough to accept us as we are, but too much to leave us that way. This is a simple truth illustrated many times in the Bible.

Jesus saw people not as losers, but as potential winners who had lost their way. When He encountered them, He was moved with compassion for them (Mark 6:34). He saw them through God's eyes—not as weeds, but as flowers. His perspective and interaction with them brought out the best in them. He focused on potential, not problems; He saw possibilities for change. In a woman with five failed marriages, Jesus saw a bruised heart longing for change, a woman who could become a restored sinner and the first evangelist. Where others saw a blind man, He focused on his longing for light and caused him to see as a merciful gift. In a reviled tax collector, He saw a future disciple. In Zacchaeus, a crook, Jesus recognized a searching heart. Where others saw an impulsive fisherman by the name of Simon,

19

Jesus saw his potential to become a leader, renamed Peter, who would build His church.

And then there was the shepherd boy, named David, in whom God saw potential. He made him a king. The Old Testament says, "For I know the plans I have for you, declares the Lord, plans to prosper you and not to harm you, plans to give you a hope and a future" (Jer. 29:11). The creator God was pouring out the same heart through His Son, Jesus Christ, when He walked among people in New Testament times just as He does today.

Dear friend, ponder for a moment these different encounters with Christ. In each of these cases, He touched hearts with compassion and hope and transformed lives. I remember the Bill Gaither song: "He touched me, O He touched me, and O the joy that floods my soul; something happened and now I know, He touched me and made me whole." Another song by Bill Gaither comes to mind: "Something beautiful, something good, all my confusion He understood, all I had to offer Him was brokenness and strife, but He made something beautiful of my life." Those are my songs as well. When Christ touches a life, there is transformation. God lets us know that He has plans for us and that we do have a future and a hope (Jer. 29:11). He lets us know He believes in us and boasts of what we can become.

One night Jesus was having dinner at the house of Matthew, the tax collector. Many other tax collectors and sinners and the disciples joined in the feast. "When the Pharisees saw this, they asked his disciples: 'Why does your teacher eat with tax collectors and sinners?' On hearing this, Jesus said: 'It is not the healthy who need a doctor but the sick. But go and learn what this means: I desire mercy not sacrifice. For I have not come to call the righteous but sinners,'" (Matt. 9:11–13). God is in the business of transformation for all those who are open to receiving His mercy, no questions asked about the past.

When I became a child of God, I was filled with hope for change. I loved and often recited 2 Corinthians 5:17: "If anyone is in Christ, he or she is a new creation, the old has gone. The new has come." Here is that same verse from the Amplified Bible: "Therefore if a person is (engrafted) in Christ, the Messiah, he is (a new creation altogether), a new creation; the old (previous moral and spiritual condition) has passed away. Behold the fresh and new has come (Amp. 2 Cor. 5:17)." Scholars tell us *new* in this passage does not mean made over, revamped, or improved upon, but entirely new and different. These truths lifted my heart with thankfulness and great hope. He was boasting of what I could become, and He let me know He believed in a new and better me.

Yes, a relationship with God is about change, and we enter a process of transformation. No wonder this is true, with a new set of spiritual DNA and new truth on which we can meditate, and which we can absorb and put into practice. Internalizing these truths leads to reprogramming our minds, just as a computer is programmed with new data. New thoughts lead to new feelings and inclinations, which lead to new actions and habits that result in a new, more Christ-like character. We become a new creation, just as He said.

Can you see that salvation is followed by transformation? How do the following scriptures give you hope for change? How does God express belief in a new you and boast of what you will become in partnership with Him?

Read 2 Corinthians 5:17 and 21 and 1 Peter 2:24 and write the verses in your own words.

This, friends, is change because of the great exchange. It is time to take God at His word and make choices that align with your new nature and identity as a child of God.

The most exciting and powerful argument for transformation is the "new creation" based on His original creation of men. In Genesis 1:27, we are told God created us in His image. This means we are God's image bearers. We have personhood, mind, emotion, and will, just like He does. And though sin has corrupted that image, Christ's cleansing blood, shed on the cross, makes it possible to become just that: God's image bearers. God is committed to restoring us to His intended design and reproducing the character of His Son and His love in us. He laid the groundwork at the creation.

What does it mean that you and I are created in His image?

How does 2 Corinthians 3:18 restate that God's children are His image bearers?

Remember, animals were created each after their own kind. The human family was created in God's image. We are the God-kind of created beings. He has a divine purpose for us. Remember that in Acts 17:28–29, we are called His offspring.

> Read Romans 8:29. As God conforms you to the image of His Son, what aspects of yourself are changed?

> Read 2 Peter 1:3–4 and express it in your own words. Can you see how committed God is to making you into His image bearer, and how He backs the promise with His power?

Does it not amaze and fill you with awe that you are a partaker of God's divine nature? Do you feel honored, lifted up, and elevated to a completely new status as His offspring? Does that realization not compel you to live up to God's pronouncements about you? Don't you want to shout for joy and excitement? Can you hear God boasting about you? Do you realize He is forming a new identity in you? You are a unique treasure to Him and a holy person belonging to Him. How can a father possibly boast more about his children? Our Heavenly Father believes in and boasts about you; He sees you far differently than how you see yourself. In this love relationship, He calls you "His child" (John 1:12). Christ calls you "His friend" (John 15:13–15). We are His "chosen people, a unique treasure, a royal priesthood, belonging to God" (2 Pet. 2:9). He truly lifts our heads when He promises to bestow glory on us, and thus our desire grows to honor Him with our lives (Ps. 3:3).

Since we live out of our identity, there is a vital connection between how we feel about ourselves and our resulting behavior. Do you see yourself as honored by your Heavenly Father and victorious in Christ or as victimized by the past? Satan loves to keep you hostage to the old identity programming and in bondage to the old sin-scarred self-image. Realize that how you view yourself will determine your response and the outcome of interactions and circumstances. We don't only view our world through these persona lenses and define ourselves by the names given to us, but they strongly define our feelings about ourselves, our actions, and our responses.

"We respond to our environment according to the way we see ourselves. Words spoken to us become names that we carry in our hearts. These names paint a portrait of us in our imagination and become the lenses through which we view our world. It is important that we live by our God-given names. And not by names that tie us to bondage. We must break free of all aliases that we have been given by the world" (Vallotton and JohnsonVallotton and Johnson, 2006, 62–63).

My friend, become rooted and anchored in how God sees you! **Can you even contain your joy and thankfulness for how your Heavenly Father boasts about and believes in what you are and still can become as His child?** He is truly the wind beneath our wings. Let us cooperate with His Spirit to lift us up to new and never-explored heights, bringing glory to His name and blessing upon blessing in our lives.

II. Believe in and Boast of What Others Can Become

One of the most important things we can do for others is to believe in them in spite of failures and appearances that infuse doubt. The famous love chapter, 1 Corinthians 13, reminds us that love is patient and kind, always protects, always trusts, always hopes, and always perseveres. We can be the wind beneath others' wings and help them rise from their past and present shortcomings and failures to become different people and overcome all odds.

Stories abound about lives that were impacted because someone saw untapped potential and planted rays of hope, spoke words of encouragement and support, and gave opportunities for change. A few years ago, a movie called *The Blind Side*, about a high school boy named Michael, was released. He was an African American with no home and little education. A woman met Michael on the street, helpless and homeless. She welcomed him into her home and family. She showered him with gracious love and supported him to graduate from high school. College at the University of Mississippi was his next step of success. Ultimately he became a well-known athlete. A hopeless life was changed through a loving relationship.

God uses the encouraging words, actions, and attitudes we direct at others to bring hope and strengthen their resolve to succeed. Abraham Lincoln was known to have practiced this kind of encouragement. It was said that wherever deserved, he made others feel great. After he died, people felt they diminished in size. I still remember the tremendous difference a teacher's stated belief in me made when I was just starting high school. We had moved to the city from the country. In clothing, speech, looks, and confidence, I had very little in common with the city girls. I felt stifled by intimidation and saw little chance of fitting into this new, competitive world. My teacher saw my potential and infused confidence in me with words of encouragement, inspiring me to give this new experience my best effort and to honor her trust.

I also remember stories of a grandfather who used every blunder or mistake not as a reason to blame his grandchild, but to encourage the child to learn and grow from the mistake, and to become better and stronger and more confident. He assured his grandchild that every mistake was a learning experience and the foundation for doing things better next time. Successful people do not dwell on their failure but look ahead to the next opportunity they have to succeed. Be encouraged: Failure can be our best teacher. Learn from it, and don't allow it to discourage you! Then plant those seeds of hope in another life. A friend gave me some encouraging words: "It does not matter how many times you failed, you need only to succeed once."

What does boasting about and believing in others look like? Trying to see the potential in others that God sees and helping them to get anchored in those truths are vital. These actions help generate a positive, hopeful attitude. Just as in God's relationship with us, believing in another person is a powerful tool for change and transformation. Building others up and supporting them in their efforts are key aspects. Aim at progress, not perfection, by pointing to and encouraging every effort in the right direction. **Focusing on potential, not problems**, will help you foster an affirming attitude and encouraging words.

Do you hear Paul describe this supportive and encouraging attitude in 1 Corinthians 13:7? **"If you love someone you will be loyal to him no matter what the cost.** You will always believe in him, always expect the best of him, and always stand your ground in defending him" (1 Cor. 13:7, TLB). Being loved by a spouse with such a supportive, affirming love sends the other spouse confidently into the "dog-eat-dog world" out there. Here are the thoughts of one lucky recipient of such a believing and boasting love: I love my wife not only for who she is, but for who I am when I am with her.

Loving our children or friends with that same affirming love braces them to stand against bullies in school and society. **Such love is the great enabler**. Honest, affirming communication, a supportive attitude, and helpful actions are our most powerful tools.

What are the four commands in Ephesians 4:29?

The Living Bible puts this verbal affirmation in simple, descriptive terms: "Don't use bad language. Say only what is good and helpful to those you are talking to, and what will give them a blessing" (Eph. 4:29, TLB). Echoing the same truths, my grandmother often cautioned, "If you have nothing good to say, don't say anything!"

Read Proverbs 12:18. What does it state about recklessness of the tongue?

Read Ephesians 4:15, and restate it in your own words.

Affirmation does not preclude honesty and possibly correction. Constructive criticism is certainly acceptable when we truly care for the other individual and express it in a tactful manner with the goal of lovingly redirecting the thoughts or actions of others. "Instead we will lovingly follow the truth at all times—speaking truly, dealing truly, living truly—and so become more and more in every way like Christ" (Eph. 4:15, TLB).

Remember, it takes time to listen with your heart and tune into another individual's life. Remember how fragile the confidence of a struggling individual can be. Every word and every action has the power to build or destroy. One careless negative comment can cancel a series of efforts toward affirmation. I have heard it said that it takes seven positive comments to undo one careless, hurtful remark. Often wounds are left that will always fester! People and circumstances can push us down, but godly, supportive love from another individual is God's instrument to bring hope and transformation.

III. Principles of Transformation

True transformation begins with a new birth when we receive God's Spirit life. It is followed by infiltration and reprogramming of our minds with God's truth (Rom. 12:1–2). Living out these truths obediently in daily life can only happen with the power of God's Spirit. We accomplish little by merely improving the flesh. That is at best a temporary change. We must learn to flex our spiritual muscles. In partnership with God, we must accept His encouraging and boasting love and likewise extend it to others as an act of obedience often contrary to our feelings. I often hear the comment, "I have God's truth in my head, but not my heart." That is just not enough. **Only truth acted on becomes life changing.** Obedience and God's Spirit power are needed when seeking and solidifying a permanent life change. As a choice of our will, we can accept that God loves us, but we need His Spirit at work in order to experience God's love warming our heart and to love others. We can intellectually accept we are forgiven, but we must be empowered by His Spirit to feel the freedom of forgiveness and lifting of guilt. Then, in turn, we can forgive others. We do not need to be filled to know we are accepted by God, but we need to be filled to accept others.

God boasts about and believes in what we can become. "For it is God who works in you to will and to act according to his good purpose" (Phil. 2:13). We can count on Him to act on our behalf, fulfilling His good purpose for our lives and for the sake of His glory, His reputation, and the growth of His kingdom.

IV. APPLICATION

1. How have the above truths impacted your relationship with God? Do you have a new sense of hope, a different outlook

2. Is there anyone in your life to whom you need to express a more affirming, encouraging love to induce hope, courage, and a desire to change?

3. Which verse did you memorize this week?

We will never forget people who believe in us, boast of what we can become, and take an active part in that journey. They will assume a very prominent place in our lives. Their godly and practical expression of love will always generate deep thankfulness. **They are true life givers**, the kind of life that Christ promised, the abundant life (John 10:10b).

CHAPTER 4
Care When People Hurt

§

CARING IS ONE OF THE most visible expressions of love. It is a necessary part of the basic fiber of the human family and the family of God. An acrostic of the word *joy* teaches us the right priorities: *Jesus, Others, You.* Yet our human nature gravitates toward putting ourselves first. Our culture makes ample room for selfishness and self-centered behavior. No wonder we are called the "me" generation. There are some praiseworthy exceptions, but the general trend is moving more and more toward indifference and neglect. Caring means being other-minded and the willingness to be the hands and feet of Jesus, moved by the heart of God. A lack of care from our Heavenly Father is unthinkable and contrary to His character. A lack of care in the human family leads to struggles and emptiness in our relationships and the breakdown of our families, followed by the demise of our society. The warning signals are visible everywhere. The heart of God is grieved.

I. GOD'S CARING LOVE TOWARD US WHEN WE HURT

In the Old Testament, God gives us a picture of His caring love expressed in the vicarious sacrifice of Christ on the cross: "Surely He has borne our griefs (sickness, weakness and distresses) and carried our sorrows and pains (of punishment)" (Isa. 53:4a, AMP). It is with Him that we should share our hurt first and foremost. Paul clearly states the dynamics of caring and comforting in 2 Corinthians 1:3–4: "Praise be to the God and Father of our Lord Jesus Christ, the Father of compassion and the God of all comfort, **who comforts us in all our troubles, so that we can comfort those in**

any trouble, with the comfort we ourselves have received from God" (2 Cor. 1:3–4).

My favorite verse showing me God's heart is found in Matthew 11:28: "Come to me, all you that are weary and burdened, and I will give you rest." He promises to ease our burden and relieve and refresh our souls.

Read 1 Peter 5:7. What does it mean to you?

Here is the same passage quoted from the Amplified Bible: "Casting the whole of your care—all your anxieties, all your worries, all your concerns, once and for all—on Him, for He cares for you affectionately, and cares about you watchfully" (1 Pet. 5:7 Amp).

Dear friend with a hurting and burdened heart, take courage! God is listening and concerned. Christ has compassion, suffers with us, and shows empathy. He enters with us into our problems and pain and understands them. Our precious Lord invites us to pour out our scared emotions to Him, honestly and fully.

David models this invitation beautifully in Psalms. We hear him start out in Psalm 13 with a question of his tortured heart: "How long, O Lord? Will you forget me forever? How long will you hide your face from me? How long must I wrestle with my thoughts and every day have sorrow in my heart?" Hear how honestly he brings his burden to God, and in that process, his burden begins to lift. He finishes his prayer with new confidence: "But I trust in your unfailing love; my heart rejoices in your salvation. I will sing to the Lord, for He has been good to me." This pattern is repeated many times over, with assurance of the Good Shepherd's restoring the struggling soul with new hope and faith. David lets us know he reaches for His God many times each day: "Evening, morning and noon I cry out in distress and He hears my voice" (Ps. 55:17). Later, he follows with strong advice for us: "Cast your cares on the Lord and he will sustain you, he will never let the righteous fall" (Ps. 55:22). And how important it is to put that burden on His shoulders and then leave it there. **Oh, the joy and freedom that comes when we release the weight to Him.** Pouring out our hearts to God, as to a caring friend, indeed lightens our burden and starts bringing us peace. Those are the first steps toward healing and wholeness.

I remember the early days of my marriage. My husband, all of our children, and I had gone through a very difficult time before deciding to put our families together. Five children between the ages of two and six became brothers and sisters, each having lost a parent. Mistakenly, I thought our commitment to have a loving, peaceful home, for which we so desperately longed, was all we needed. However, old wounds in our hearts were still festering, and the saying "wounded people wound people" became all too true. When it became obvious our efforts and hopes had failed and everything seemed hopeless, I realized that God had indeed surrounded me with His love all the way to the bottom of the pit where I found myself.

It became all too clear that I was a miserable sinner, so very lost, defeated in my self-efforts and without hope. A compassionate and caring friend invited me to Bible study. Coming from a background where Christianity was a culture and religion, I met people who actually had a *relationship* with Jesus. That was when I accepted Jesus as Savior and Lord of my life. In the still moments at His feet, I soaked up His caring love. It was like ointment to my wounded soul. His promise in Psalms proved so true: He heals the brokenhearted and binds up their wounds (Ps. 147:3). His word gave me clear guidelines for my behavior and deeper insights into the struggles of the human heart. With these came deeper understanding of my soul, which gave me a new perspective and brought hope, as well as some resolution to our problems. In time, Christ's love brought inner healing, and I became a whole new person. He was my Shepherd, and I came to fully trust His love and goodness following me all the days of my life (Ps. 23). Daily, He taught me more about loving as He does. Ultimately, His love at work in our individual hearts and relationships gave us the marriage and home for which we all longed.

Read Psalm 23. How do you see the love of our caring Shepherd, Jesus Christ, displayed? What does He provide in that relationship? How close is He, how involved is He? Please note your answers in the space provided. It is important that you glean the truths of God's Word yourself and note them down.

What do the rod and the staff represent in His caring?

Where do you see the work of the Holy Spirit?

Examine Matthew 10:29, 12:11, and 18:12–13. How does God assure us of His personal care for each individual and His particular focus on any struggling and lost child of His?

What a picture of a personal, living God who seeks us out and walks alongside when we struggle and hurt. What do the following scriptures promise?

Deuteronomy 32:11

Psalm 147:3, one of my favorites

Job 12:10

Isaiah 40:28–31, 49:13

Matthew 20:34

All of these verses imply closeness. Beware. We, the sheep, tend to go our own way and stray from the Shepherd. Just as David modeled, we have to be willing to come into His presence to pour out our hearts and receive His touch, His love, and His strength. We have to be still to experience His goodness consciously and come to know that He loves us, His children, with a compassionate, caring love. The Bible exhorts: "Be still and know that I am God" (Ps. 46:10a). How true ring the words of one of God's special servants, Michael Wells, whom I heard at an Abiding Life Conference: **"There is nothing that the nearness of Christ cannot cure."**

There are moments in each life when Christ is all we have, the only one we can on call and depend on. We certainly find the following truth applicable to our lives: **When Christ is all we have, Christ is all we need.**

Dear friend, how very important it is, therefore, to cultivate this closeness with Him. Sometimes it is merely a discipline, an obedient choice we make. But to this I can testify: It always ends up as a love affair, a time of loving Him and feeling ever so loved by Him! As I bring my struggles to

Him, a wonderful exchange begins to take place: **My weakness for His strength** (2 Cor. 12:9).

Please give the essence of 2 Corinthians 12:9 in your own words.

Paul even goes so far as to say, "That is why, for Christ's sake, I delight in weaknesses, insults, in hardship, in persecutions, in difficulties. For when I am weak, then I am strong" (2 Cor. 12:10). This passage speaks of a deep, satisfying confidence and trust in experiencing God's hand and being the object of His caring, comforting love when the going gets rough.

II. Show Caring Love toward Others When They Hurt

This is the "me" generation. Being other-minded is becoming more and more countercultural. It is easy for our desires, our pleasures, and our concerns to govern our thoughts and our time. Yet human nature has not changed, just our culture. We still need each other, particularly when we hurt. Caring love finds many expressions: compassionate listening; an encouraging smile; carefully chosen words; a warm, steady hug; and an offer to help in practical ways. These efforts are seldom refused and always minister to the struggles of the soul. We use different terms: support, encouragement, understanding, sympathy, empathy, and compassion.

In 2 Corinthians 1:3–4, Paul tells us: "Praise be to the God and Father of our Lord Jesus Christ, the Father of Compassion and the God of all comfort, who comforts us in all our troubles, so that we can comfort those in any trouble with the comfort **we ourselves received from God.**"

God models a caring, comforting love. He ministers to us in that way. As we have received comfort, we must now let it flow out. I know we always feel blessed being on the receiving end, but are we ready to care and to give? Often, our fears of getting involved and the constraints of not needing another burden or not having enough time keep us from following His example. Repeatedly, Christ, knowing our hearts and struggle, asks the question, "Do you have compassion?"

Just as with God, listening is a key element of caring. That is, listening not just with our ears, but with our hearts. This kind of listening allows us to hear the heart cry expressed beyond the words and to assess the true need. Often, compassionate listening is all that is needed to show we care. "Fixing" is many times not required, and sometimes not even desired. My friend, don't you agree that being heard when you express pain, hurt, and concerns lightens the load? Is this not what the Lord reminds us in Matthew 11:28?

While we should go first to God with our hurts, we often feel the need for a hug from another person, sympathetic eyes to look into, and to hear someone say, "**We can handle this together.**" I am reminded of Christ in the garden the night before the crucifixion, when He urged His disciples to stay awake with Him "to watch and pray" (Mark 14:34–38). He wanted for them to enter with Him into His suffering. We call that "having empathy" and showing compassion toward others. And, my friend, if Christ needed it, how much more needy are we in our broken humanity?

Look at the following verses and express the essence in your own words: Romans 15:1–2.

Do you see another exchange of weakness for strength, this time drawing on your strength? Do you find this difficult? Remember that Paul drew on the strength of Christ in his weakness. In this exchange, we allow a weakened individual who needs support and encouragement to draw on our strength.

Do you ever struggle with not wanting to get involved? Explain why.

At times, caring goes beyond listening and requires greater involvement, just as the shepherd walks alongside the struggling sheep and helps a helpless sheep get back on its feet. To what do the following verses allude? Galatians 6:2a in the Amplified Bible translation commands, "Bear, endure, carry one another's burdens and troublesome moral faults, and in this way fulfill and observe perfectly the law of Christ."

What promise follows in Galatians 6:9?

Many times, I have lost heart and grown weary in doing good. It taught me that supporting a struggling friend is not a short sprint, but can seem more like a marathon. To see that friend overcome the struggle and walk steadily once again is our reward, and the words of our Heavenly Father—"Well done my faithful servant"—bless our soul.

Put the command in 1 John 3:18 into your own words.

Also look at James 2:15–20, 26. What is a necessary and practical expression of our faith?

Read Isaiah 58:6–11. List the commands.

List God's promises of blessings for those who care in word and deed.

In summary, the following is a suggested sequence of caring expressions and actions:

1. Listening prayerfully with the heart and showing compassion.
2. Being willing to tune in to others' suffering and expressing empathy.
3. Entering into a meaningful discussion and allowing them to verbalize their struggle. Validate their feelings. Remember, feelings are not always true, logical, right, or wrong, but they are real to those struggling. Validate their struggle. You might never struggle with that same issue. We are all individuals. Pious advice or assurance of prayers often brings little relief.
4. **Shedding light from God's Word on the issue and bringing comforting truth**. Help them see "the other side" of the issue and put things into perspective. Realize that the way we experience life is often 10 percent of what happens to us and 90 percent of how we read it. This means that our hurt sometimes has more to do with our interpretation and perception than with the actual offense.
5. Praying with them and staying with the situation to bring assurance and encouragement.
6. If possible, walking alongside them toward a resolution. Give practical help and support as warranted.
7. Encouraging them, praying for them, staying in contact, and following up.

III. Principles at Work

The "as" principle—as in "comfort as I do" from 2 Corinthians 1:3–4—has already been discussed.

Now, we take up the "react versus respond" principle. **It involves looking into our own as well as the other individual's heart.**

Sometimes, when others share their hurt or struggle, we are part of the problem. In response, we can either react or respond to what we hear or feel coming toward us. We often react out of fear, anger, or self-defense. If the issue that caused the injury relates to something we have said or done, it is not easy to lend a compassionate or even a patient ear. Instead, we tend to justify, defend, explain, or lash out in anger or self-defense: "Wounded people wound people."

My friend, it is time to become part of the solution! To soften hearts and get the communication going, it is important to confess our own part in the conflict, as warranted. Matthew gives good advice: "You hypocrite, first take the plank out of your own eye, then you will see clearly to remove the speck from your brother's eye" (Matt. 7:5). This act of honesty and humility opens the channels of communication. These might be words of regret over our own actions or lack of sensitivity. This humble acknowledgment of our perceived wrong will deflate anger and tension and lead to a fruitful exchange. Maybe it is time to cede some ground! That certainly shows understanding, often softens hearts, and shows goodwill. Also check out Matthew 5:21–23. Here we are instructed to deal with the conflict and seek reconciliation. This is a definite part of caring love that seeks to minister to hurt and to resolve conflicts. A simple word of advice helps greatly to control our reactions and channel our emotion toward a helpful response: Don't see the deed or react to the words. **Focus instead on the needs of that individual**, expressed in actions or words.

That is why Paul talks about speaking words of encouragement to meet their needs (Eph. 4:29). This becomes possible if we allow God to meet our own needs first in the relationship with Him. **The emphasis is on meeting their needs and caring because they hurt**. This response can happen only if we seek a deeper understanding of their feelings and meet them there. It is helpful to extend assurance, forgiveness, encouragement, grace, or tenderness. Possibly, a renewed commitment to the relationship needs to be expressed. Maybe wrong actions or the perception of wrong actions or indifference needs to be acknowledged. These conciliatory actions open hearts toward us and give the possibility of a healthy exchange. As a result, we work together toward a deeper understanding of and solutions to the conflict and hurt. People almost always respond to caring love, humility, and fairness. They soften when we affirm them as a person and consider the relationship more important than the issue at hand. It touches their heart to see that we care about the relationship and are willing to become vulnerable in an effort to restore it.

This caring exchange leads ultimately to lessening of the conflict. It lightens their burden and helps them walk toward constructive solutions. It ushers **peace into the relationship and allows God's Spirit to infuse restorative powers.** People feel valued, and they are assured that they are not alone, isolated, or abandoned. Our love ministers to them, and they experience a caring community after God's design and heart.

IV. Application

1. Write out and memorize 1 Peter 5:7.

2. Look at Ephesians 4:31–32. How does God's admonition in this verse help you respond rather than react to another person?

3. How has God's caring love touched and changed your inner world?

4. Think of a specific relationship that needs healing. In what ways can you show this person you care?

5. Which communication skills do you need to work on?

6. Think of a specific trigger situation in your daily life where you need to respond instead of react.

7. What does "ministering to their need" mean in a specific situation with which you currently struggle?

CHAPTER 5
Desire and Do the Best for Others

THIS SEEMS HARD TO DO at times. Getting and giving in our relationships are mostly defined by what is "deserved." Have you ever wondered how much of what we do is purely motivated by the goodness of our hearts and not calculated to work to our advantage? Thankfully, the heart of God operates in stark contrast to our human nature. There is no greater comfort than knowing that our Heavenly Father indeed desires and does the best for us, and this is in spite of who we are and what we do. "The Lord is gracious and compassionate, slow to anger and rich in love. The Lord is good to all; He has compassion on all He has made. The eyes look to you, and you give them their food at the proper time. You open your hand and satisfy the desires of every living thing. The Lord is righteous in all His ways and loving toward all He has made" (Ps. 146:8–9, 15–17).

Friend, do you remember the wonderful, comforting verses from Psalm 23? "Surely goodness and love will follow me all the days of my life, and I will dwell in the house of the Lord forever" (Ps. 23:6).

I. GOD DESIRING AND DOING THE BEST FOR US IN THE LOVE RELATIONSHIP WITH HIM

Mercy: not getting the punishment we deserve.

Mercy—loving-kindness—describes the heart of our Creator God. Used over thirty times in the Old Testament alone, the word *mercy* states a truth about our Heavenly Father that no other religion in the world can claim. These next verses are probably familiar to you. They represent the heart of the Gospel, God's good news for all of humanity.

Look up Romans 3:23 and 6:23 and finish the following sentences:

For all have...

The wages of sin is death, but...

So what do we deserve from God's perspective? We deserve death, both spiritual and physical, and life under the curse of sin, with its terrible consequences for each life, for each moment, for time and eternity. But our God is a God of love and mercy, which define His nature and actions (1 John 4:16). Do you remember the definition of love? **"Giving people what they need most, when they deserve it least, at personal sacrifice."**

The familiar truths of John 3:16 summarize the only salvation and hope for any and every person walking this earth, including me: "For God so loved you and me, that He gave His one and only Son, that if I believe in Him, I will not perish but have eternal life" (John 3:16).

So I ask you, my friend. Do we deserve God's goodness toward us? We certainly do not. But, praises be to God, it is His character, His nature, and His unchangeable purpose for all humanity that determine His actions toward us.

God is love. His nature is full of love, kindness, mercy, righteousness, and faithfulness. He created us to be in a relationship with Him (Ps. 89:14). His desire and plan are to restore all of humanity and all of creation to their original purpose, to experience the fullness of His goodness.

How do Jeremiah 9:23 and 24 express the importance of knowing and understanding the above truths?

Do you think it is important for us to know the character of God? Why or why not?

It is because of His righteousness and justice that God gave us His Son to become the sacrificial lamb and pay the penalty for our sins. Christ died the death we should have died so that we can live the life we are destined to live. It is because of His loving-kindness and mercy that He withholds the punishment we deserve and makes us the recipients of His goodness.

Now, think back to the definition of love and the aspect of giving that love at a personal cost. We already talked about God giving His Son. The Son Himself also gave and paid a costly price.

What does Philippians 2:5–7 tell us about Christ's sacrifice?

Think of His agony on the cross, carrying the full burden of the world's sins, to the point where He felt completely abandoned by God. We will never understand the inexpressible pain of His words: "My God, my God, why have You forsaken me?" (Mark 15:34).

How can we ever fail to see that God indeed desires to do and give His very best for us? **This immeasurable gift is available to all—every man, woman, and child—but needs to be received by a humble and repentant heart.** Look up the following verses and let them speak to your heart:

Romans 2:4b

John 1:12

Lamentations 3:22

Ephesians 2:4

Because of these truths and promises from God's Word, we thank Him deeply, boldly hoping and expecting that He will do and desire the best for us in that relationship and partnership with Him. It is His character that guarantees the keeping of His promises. Our faith believes in those promises, and His continued mercy allows His goodness to flow freely from His hand of grace to us. Desiring the best for us goes beyond withholding what we deserve and finds a continued expression in loving-kindness toward us.

II. Loving-Kindness: The Goodness of God toward Us

Jesus Christ has become the tool and vessel through which our Father God has shown His redeeming love toward us. The Son summarized these truths most powerfully: **"I have come that they may have life and have it to the full"** (John 10:10b). He talks about eternal life, as well as the abundant life, here and now: "Christ gave His life for me, to give His life to me, to live His life through me. In His great love for us He has given us a new birth into a living hope" (1I Pet. 1:3). So, dear friend, you see He has poured out the life of His Son for you. Now open your heart so He can pour out His goodness into your life. In Jeremiah 29:11, God makes a bold statement that infuses hope into any anxious and discouraged heart: "I know the plans I have for you, declares the Lord, plans to prosper you, and not to harm you, plans to give you hope and a future," (Jer. 29:11).

Can you sense how involved God wants to be in *your* life? Does that give you hope, confidence, trust, and anticipation of what He and you can do together?

There will be change. There will be healing, wholeness, satisfaction, joy, peace, sound relationships, and productivity. If we live the vine life—that means abiding in Him, remaining in Him, making our home in Him—there will be abundance. Abundance is not the best of health or wealth, but the ability to deal with life's situations productively, with His guidance and empowerment, toward the best possible outcome, because of our relationship with Him.

State the promise of Ephesians 3:20 in your own words.

Do you truly believe that He will do exceedingly, abundantly more than you ask or think? In what specific difficult aspect of your life do you trust God to do His best for you and through you right now?

In Ephesians 3:19, Paul describes God's love as surpassing all knowledge so that we might be filled to the measure of all the fullness of God. What do you think? Is God running on a small budget with His love and goodness toward you? No. We have all of it, including

His power to work out life's challenges in our best interests, fulfilling His good purpose for us. I also love Romans 15:13. Why do you think hope, joy, and His power are so important as we face our daily challenges?

Remember that God's love toward us does not involve just a set of good wishes or desires, but actually giving his best, the life of His Son. Christ in turn gave up His best, to restore each one of us to our God-given potential and purpose so that we could become our best.

III. Desire and Do the Best in Your Relationships

"Clothe yourselves with tenderhearted mercy, kindness, humility, gentleness, and patience...above all clothe yourselves with love, which binds us all together in perfect harmony" (Col. 3:12a, 14b NLT).

Now, my friend, hang on to the understanding of the heart of God. We talked about His mercy, withholding what we deserve, and, because of His loving-kindness, letting His goodness flow toward us instead. And then be ready to receive His command: "Be merciful just as your Father is merciful" (Luke 6:36). Now look at this verse in the context of the biblical definition of love: "Giving others what they need most, when they deserve it least, at personal sacrifice."

As we talk about desiring and doing the best for others as an expression of godly love, our behavior should show the above characteristics: withholding what others deserve and instead pouring out the goodness of our hearts in their best interests, even at some personal cost. Yes, that is it! Wow, where do we see this happening? Talk about being countercultural and revolutionary. I have to shamefully confess that there are times when I almost feel satisfaction when someone who has wronged others or me seems to get some payback. There is that little ugly voice that whispers, "He or she had it coming." This ugliness of my human heart conflicts with God's kind of love: desiring and doing the best for individuals in spite of their actions toward me. In James 2:13, we have clear guidelines: Mercy triumphs over judgment. Here are Christ's own words: "Blessed are the merciful for they will be shown mercy" (Matt. 5:7).

Showing mercy is by no means always easy, nor does it come naturally to us. Yet, as we looked at God modeling this aspect of love for us, one thing is clear. **It is not about getting what we deserve, but what God commands us to do**: to love as He loves. Do you see a problem? Yes, certainly, if we do what comes easily or naturally, we give tit for tat, are selfish and indifferent, treat others as we have been treated, and try not to get involved. Yet His command is to love as He loves.

Honestly, friend, at times I find myself just in sheer rebellion: "No way," my mind screams. Other times I humbly confess, "Lord, I just can't do that. I just don't have any goodness to give." God's solution: ***His* character and nature express themselves through us**. That is how He empowers His children to walk in His ways.

There were times in my life when I ran low on patience or when I was just too exhausted to serve my family one more time. There were times when I really did not have it in me to submit to my husband, while not at all agreeing with his course of action. Yet he needed my support, and God expects me to be his "helpmate." Just recently I faced such a situation, and it was as if the Lord whispered to me, "You either become part of the problem or the solution." Desiring and doing the best for my husband in this particular situation became a challenge that seemed bigger than I was. In my own good judgment, the course of action was just wrong! It was at the end of a long journey of trials and challenges relating to the same issue. During all of those situations, there was one choice of action that really helped. Going to the Lord with my struggle, I told Him, "Lord, I just don't have it within me, but there is nothing that You cannot handle. Please let Your life flow through me to help me be patient, to support, serve, and love. I just don't have it myself." And, dear struggling friend, He has never let me down.

Read Galatians 2:20, and put these amazing truths into your own words.

Understanding and living out Galatians 2:20 made a radical difference in my life. It offset my inabilities with Christ's ability, my struggle with His empowerment and direction. Desiring and doing the best for others thus becomes a lifestyle that we must choose to enter. Our goal must become to do what is in their best interest.

God leaves no doubt in our minds that godly love is sacrificial. Just as it is said about Christ in Matthew 20:28 and Mark 10:45: "The Son of man did not come to be served but to serve." **Loving involves being a servant. It puts hands and feet to our goal of desiring and doing the best for others, whether they deserve it or not.**

Give an example of how this verse might translate to your life: "Serve one another in godly love" (Gal. 5:13b).

It was very helpful to me as a young mother of five children to come with that mind-set to my daily tasks. It made the burden of a hard day lighter and more satisfying. My focus was to do the best for my children. While there was mostly little recognition by others, I often felt God's words—"Well done my good and faithful servant" (Matt. 5:23)—fall on my heart after an exhausting day. Being in the business of building young lives became an honor and a privilege. God has rewarded us with good fruit. We are proud of our children. Achieving good things, even great things, involves a servant spirit. As Jesus said, "Whoever wants to become great among you must be your servant" (Matt. 25:21). **If we want to be loving and caring parents, spouses, friends, leaders, and people who impact other lives positively, we need to be willing to serve by desiring and doing the best for others**.

That often requires putting the goals and needs of others first. It means being aware of the challenges and setbacks they experience. It necessitates becoming their source of hope and confidence, demonstrated by our attitude and actions. It implies that we help others win and are happy to take an assist. We do our best to give them a chance and help them score. We rejoice with those who rejoice and feel blessed to humbly share in their victories. As authentic leaders, we accept responsibility and are hesitant to assign blame.

There are times when relationships cause us a lot of pain. Desiring the best for a loved one is difficult when we have been offended, hurt, rejected, or violated in that relationship. The gut reaction in our flesh is anger, the urge to push back and pay back in like manner and to seek revenge. Ill will is quickly generated when relationships become stressful and interactions are depleting. Yet what is God's clear instruction?

What is the essence of Matthew 5:44–46?

Loving our enemies and praying for those who persecute us is difficult. Yet it is the very thing that melts the icy coldness of hearts. It authenticates us as God's children. It frees us to work toward restoration in our relationships. Why is it so important to clear offenses and make things right? Even in the family of God, relational problems can cause heartaches and division. Those times when my heart is parched and bent toward ugly and negative feelings and actions, I can take full comfort in knowing that God is completely aware of my struggle. Yes, my friend, it is just plain hard to desire and do the best for someone undeserving of goodness. Yet, as long as my conscience is tender and bent toward seeking the good of the other individual, my Lord Jesus Christ is glad to receive my cry to love through me and show me how to best deal with this situation to bring honor to His name.

> How does Romans 12:9–21 address this issue? Make a list of the dos and don'ts in this passage.

> Does God's assurance that He is the judge, that He will avenge and repay, make it easier to overcome evil with good (Rom. 12:17–19)? Why?

Isn't it good to know that God uses our very desire and effort to do the best for others to cause His Spirit to convict them of their wrong against us? This implies that our releasing the other individual of the wrong against us frees God's Spirit to go to work.

God summarizes a difficult command of loving the unlovable: **"Do not be overcome by evil but overcome evil with good"** (Rom. 12:21). It takes nothing less than His nature of loving-kindness and mercy to fill our starved hearts and act with love against the natural inclinations of our hearts.

Once again we can see how this aspect of love is built on the foundation and example of God's relationship with us, His children. God uses His mercy and goodness toward us to convict us of sin rather than to simply condemn us. He compels us with His love. See how clearly Paul states this in Romans 2:4b: "God's kindness leads us toward repentance." **Likewise, He uses our kindness toward others to bring conviction to their hearts and godly sorrow.**

This is particularly important when individuals have fallen out of fellowship with the family of God and even with God Himself. Judgment toward them brings isolation and can lead to them completely falling away from God and coming to despair. I am thinking of the words of Job: "A despairing man should have the devotion of his friends, even if he forsakes the fear of the Almighty" (Job 6:14). Sadly, the Christian community is known for shooting its wounded. Our kindness—desiring and doing the best for them and infusing hope and grace into the situation—could mean a turnaround and a pathway to repentance, a new beginning, and a changed life. Indeed, we are God's agents of restoration.

IV. The Principle of Multiplied Return

Lack of acknowledgment of our kindness toward another individual may become discouraging. During those times, it is good to know that God always sees our deeds. I found that God blesses me many times more than I bless others. Put the following scriptures into your own words:

Ecclesiastes 11:1

Luke 6:38

There are times we feel that we have little to give toward the good of others. God encourages us to give what we can and to give obediently and graciously. Then He will take what we give and multiply it, just as He did the small portion of flour and oil from the widow of Zarephath (1 Kings 17:7–15). As a result, God met not only Elijah's need but also that of the widow and her son with an unending supply of flour and oil. God took the little she had to give and multiplied it.

Likewise, God honors our limited love that honestly desires the best for others and our willingness to participate in bringing it about. In return, He pours blessings on our lives. We can never out-give God.

The more we lose ourselves in something bigger than ourselves, the larger our heart capacity grows and the more energized we become. Experts tell us it is one of the best ways to diffuse thoughts of tiredness and even depression. **More important, dear friend, there is no more powerful witness for the Gospel and our faith than the expression of sacrificial, undeserved love, because it mirrors God's heart to others.** As we desire and do the best for others, we walk out our faith in the practical challenges of daily life.

V. Application

1. Pick one verse that has spoken particularly to your heart. Write the verse and memorize it.

2. Which verse was most meaningful to you in Romans 12:20–21? Why?

3. Did you ever receive a special return of blessings because you gave? What motivated your actions?

4. Why is it countercultural in today's society to desire the best for others?

5. Can you think of a time when God multiplied what you gave in love and even returned the blessing back to your life? How did that make you feel?

CHAPTER 6

Walk in Forgiveness and Freedom

Nothing in our relationship with God or others weighs us down more heavily than a sin not confessed and guilt or offenses with which we have not dealt. Hanging on to the weight of guilt and a slew of negative feelings hampers our journey of faith. The bondage of emotional bruises easily leads to festering anger against the one who wronged us. It breeds a hard and unforgiving spirit, a bitter burden of plotting vengeance, or even hate. These struggles hold us captive. They affect and destroy us spiritually, emotionally, and physically. Not experiencing God's forgiveness or extending forgiveness to others is used by Satan to rob us of God's divine purpose and intended freedom. Instead we become prisoners of our own inner distorted and sinful world.

I. A Journey toward Freedom

Paul boldly declares our Lord's intent: **"It is for freedom that I have set you free"** (Gal. 5:1). Therefore God commands us to set aside the old yoke of slavery imposed by the law but now, motivated by grace, choose to put aside the sins that so easily entangle us to be able to run the race set before us effectively (Heb. 12:1).

For years I have made the words of Psalm 139:23–24 an important part of my daily prayers. I still recommend it for daily upkeep of our inner world: "Search me, oh God, and know my heart; test me and know my anxious thoughts, and see if there is any offensive way in me, and lead me in the way everlasting."

Friend, we need to ask God to lay bare all the negative, destructive feelings that hold us captive. The first recorded words of Jesus Christ defining His mission here on earth were spoken on a Sabbath day in the synagogue: "The Spirit of the Lord is on me, because He has anointed me to preach good news to the poor. He has sent me to proclaim freedom for the prisoners and recovery of sight for the blind, to release the oppressed, and to proclaim the year of the Lord's favor" (Luke 4:18–19).

Struggles with guilt, sin, and wrongs with which we have not dealt make us prisoners of the resulting emotions and continue to oppress us. Satan uses those dynamics to disable us in our relationship with God and others. He causes defeat and hopes we stray from our Christian walk. God's plan and purpose is to set us on a journey of forgiveness and freedom. **It begins with humbly coming to our Father God with a spirit tuned in to His Spirit, a heart ready to be touched, and a mind receptive to His truth.**

II. God Erases All Offenses in His Relationship with Us

God's forgiveness of our offenses against Him, which the Bible calls sin, and the cleansing through the blood of Jesus open the door that leads to a relationship with our Heavenly Father. This unspeakable privilege is an expression of His love and grace to all of humanity. My friend, how I praise Him for my relationship with Him!

Read Colossians 1:13–14. What did God do for us?

Redemption means that God gave the life of His Son to rescue us, to purchase us back from Satan's domain. Read Ephesians 1:3–8 and summarize these promises in your own words.

Being able to trust in God's ongoing, faithful, and forgiving love makes me feel safe in that relationship with Him. However, even the journey of a child of God is marked by sin and failure. How reassuring is His promise that when I do wrong as a child of God and come to Him in repentance seeking His forgiveness, He is faithful and just to forgive me (1 John 1:9). Cleansing and erasing my offenses gives me a clean slate. The result is restoration of intimacy in my relationship with Him, which puts peace in my conscience and heart, confidence in my prayer life, and His empowerment in my walk as a child of God (1 John 3:21–22). The penalty for my wrong has already been paid for on the cross. Coming humbly before Him assures me of His forgiveness, which is already granted because of His shed blood. I am able to rest and trust in that, freed from guilt. That is vital because guilt builds walls, and Satan uses that sense of separation to defeat us as believers. We *must not* grant him that option.

Follow the steps of conviction, confession, and forgiveness that lifted the weight of guilt and brought restoration in David's life. Listen to a child of God called a man after God's heart (1 Sam. 13:14, Acts 13:33).

David pours out his penitent heart and guilty conscience to God: "According to your unfailing love, according to your great compassion blot out my transgressions, wash away all my iniquity and cleanse me from my sin" (Ps. 51:1–2).

He trusts in God's gracious, forgiving, and cleansing love: "*Cleanse* me with hyssop, and I will be clean; *wash* me and I will be whiter than snow. Hide your face from my sins and *blot out* all my iniquities" (Ps. 51:7, 9, emphasis added).

He anxiously anticipates freedom from the crushing weight of sin: "*Let me hear joy* and gladness, let the bones you have crushed rejoice" (Ps. 51:8, emphasis added).

He pleads for restoration of the close relationship with God and the power of His Spirit: "Do not cast me from our presence or take our Holy Spirit from me" (Ps. 51:11–12). He prays for God to restore the joy of his salvation and to renew a steadfast spirit within him.

Now read Psalm 32:1–5. How does David express the blessedness and freedom of forgiveness?

Can you sense his relief and freedom of heart and soul? Do you know the peace of a cleansed conscience? Look at all the action words in the previous verses.

In scripture David is called "a man after God's own heart." Why?

What sequence of steps dealing with sin do you see in 1 John 1:9? Compare them to David's words in Psalm 51. What are the key elements in both passages? Do you think those elements are essential in dealing with sin before God in our lives?

Now, my friend, thankfully receive the awesome promises God makes in Psalm 103: "Praise the Lord, oh my soul, and forget none of His benefits—who *forgives all* of our sins. For as high as the heavens are above the earth, so great is His love for those who fear Him, As far as the east is from the west, so far has *He removed* our transgressions from us" (Ps. 103:2, 3, 11, 12 emphasis added).

What does Jeremiah 31:34 mean when it says that God forgives and remembers no more?

Look at Micah 7:18–19. It really speaks to my heart: "Who is a God like you who pardons sin and forgives transgressions…you will tread our sins under foot and hurl all our iniquities into the depth of the sea."

By *all*, God means just that: all sins and failures, past, present, and future. By *removed*, He means just that: He does not hold our offenses against us anymore. He will not bring them up again. They are gone, removed as far as the east is from the west, tossed into the sea (Mic. 7:19). The sacrifice of Christ points to the cross and what it signifies: paid in full! The writer of Hebrews assures us that by that one sacrifice of Christ we have been made holy (Heb. 10:12–13). Listen to the Living Bible Translation version of Hebrews 10:17–18 and hear God's voice: "I will never again remember their sins and lawless deeds. Now, when sins have been forgiven, there is no need to offer any more sacrifices. In any legal system punishment happens only once. And that happened on the cross. My friend, do you experience the freedom God has given you from the sin burden? Nothing for you to do, it is done! So rejoice and be thankful! He sees us cleansed by the blood of Christ (1 John 1:7), and more than that, He has clothed us instead with His righteousness. "He made Him, who had no sin, to become sin for us so that in Him we might become the righteousness of God" (2 Cor. 5:21). Jesus became a curse for us (Gal. 3:13), and we received the righteousness of Christ. **What an exchange anchored in God's grace. God treats us not according to what we have been, but according to what we have received from Him.**

Pause a moment and repeat several times: "I am the righteousness of God in Christ Jesus." If you are in a group, say it to your neighbor. Begin your day speaking it back to God. Watch how it lifts your spirit!

This has been God's plan all along. Look at Isaiah 61:10 and his words of praise while claiming this promise yourself.

No wonder God boldly declares that we are a new creation in Christ, and we are free from any kind of condemnation (2 Cor. 5:17). Express the essence of this verse in a prayer of thanksgiving to God.

Write out the promise for you in Romans 8:1–2.

Dear friend, are you a prisoner set free? Which of the previous verses states most eloquently that your sins are erased and your slate is wiped clean? Have you experienced this freedom He talks about? Do you really see yourself clothed in His righteousness? Review and memorize the verses about forgiveness to make them a stronger reality in your life. This is what transforms your thinking about yourself and helps you understand the essence of God's forgiving heart (Rom. 12:1–2). My fellow sojourners in Christ, let us live in these truths and have them permeate our thoughts and feelings and transform our actions and lives.

III. REMEMBER

God cares more than anything about His relationship with us. Sin in the believer's life, though atoned for by Christ's blood, isolates our hearts from God. God's children never lose their place in the Father's heart, but sin takes away our intimacy with God and our effectiveness and power in our prayer life and Christian walk and ministry. This is why we have the promise in 1 John 1:9: Because of the cross, forgiveness and cleansing can be depended on. The penalty for sin has been paid, and that needs to happen only once. But repentance and confession clear our conscience when we do wrong and remove the burden of guilt.

To have a clear, unshaken, and blameless conscience and to guard the well-being of our soul, we need to keep short accounts with God and others. Paul made this important point in his defense before Felix: "I strive always to keep my conscience clear before God and men" (Acts 24:16). Repentance, confession, and erasing all offenses bring God's continued protection. They restore closeness and vitality to your relationship with Him. Satan knows all of this and loves seeing us with a heavy and burdened conscience. He wants to keep us carrying the burden of guilt, the disappointment of failure, and the isolation and separation that doing wrong produces in relationships. His hope is that our conscience will grow hardened and callous toward wrong. His goal is our defeat! Restoration of our relationships with God or others becomes less likely and more difficult with each day of offenses not confessed or forgiven. Just as much as Satan rejoices in our defeat, he hates victorious Christians. He comes to steal, kill, and destroy (John 10:10a). He is the great accuser of God's children before the Father's throne (Rev. 12:10). His goal is to turn us into ineffective, powerless Christians.

Here is the way to counter his attack, as demonstrated so well by Jesus Himself in His encounter with Satan in the wilderness: using the power of the Word of God (Luke 4). Each time he comes to attack and defeat you, stand ready to shoot back with a promise you claim from God's Word. Here are a few examples:

"I have confessed to the Lord. I am assured He
has cleansed and forgiven me" (1 John 1:9).

"I am in Christ Jesus, my Lord, by faith and no one or nothing can condemn me anymore. I am set free" (Rom. 8:1).

"I have been purchased by Him with His blood and my sins are forgiven" (Eph. 1:7).

"My Father in heaven has not only forgiven me, He remembers my sins no more" (Jer. 31:34).

In John 10:10, Jesus describes Satan as a thief, murderer, and destroyer of God's children. In stark contrast, Jesus talks about Himself as the life giver who desires to bring fullness and abundance into our faith walk. This is only possible if we appropriate God's forgiveness every moment of our day, by claiming and standing on His promises and walking in the freedom of His grace. Satan hates our freedom in Christ. He hopes to block the journey of repentance and forgiveness and instead pushes us toward remorse, despair, and hopelessness.

What is the constant force that moves the heart of God even when we fall or fail to meet His standards? **Yes, friend, you are right, it is His unfailing love that draws us and keeps us in Him.**

IV. APPLICATION

1. Which aspect of God's forgiving love is most precious to you?

2. Pick two verses that speak most eloquently to your need to feel cleansed and freed from guilt. Memorize them.

3. Will you commit to counter each attack from Satan with God's truth from His Word?

4. Why is it so important to keep short accounts with God and live with a clear conscience?

CHAPTER 7
Erase Offenses in Your Relationships

"Relationships don't thrive because the guilty are punished, but because the innocent are merciful" (Max Lucado, Facebook post, February 11, 2013).

JESUS COUNTS ON HIS DISCIPLES, all Christ followers, to be forgiving people. Think of the words in the Lord's Prayer taught by Jesus: "Forgive us our debts, as we also have forgiven our debtors" (Matt. 6:12). Just as being forgiven in our relationship with God is foundational, so it is critically important to forgive others in our relationship with them. The more real, personal, and carved into our hearts God's forgiveness is for us, the more readily we forgive others without keeping a record of wrongs and doing frequent replays of their offenses (1 Cor. 13:5). God's command is clear: "Be kind and compassionate to one another, forgiving each other, just as in Christ God forgave you" (Eph. 4:32).

I. WHAT MOVES AND COMPELS ME TO FORGIVE

Forgiving others is one of God's commands repeated many times in His word. The fact that God has forgiven me moves and compels my heart more than anything to extend forgiveness to others. I feel deeply loved and humbled. I rest in the completeness of that forgiveness. I also remind myself that others who have wronged me are already forgiven by God because of the shed blood of Jesus, or they can obtain forgiveness by seeking it in Jesus's name. Who am I, then, to withhold forgiveness? That seems to reflect immense arrogance and pride, a response of the flesh. Have you wondered, my friend, how God feels about this? Read Matthew 18:21–35. Christ told this parable in answer to Peter's questions about the number of times we need to forgive others.

Who is the king in this parable? Who is the first servant?

Why is the king so angered over the servant's refusal to extend grace?

When he is turned over to jailers and torturers, what do they represent?

How adamant is God about our forgiving others? Should God's forgiveness not result in deep thankfulness, humility, and a choice to act likewise toward others?

The word of God drives repeatedly into our hearts the command to forgive: "Bear with each other, and forgive whatever grievances you may have against one another. **Forgive as the Lord forgave you**" (Col. 3:13, emphasis added). Notice the repetition of the word *as*. Here is the translation from the Living Bible: "Make allowances for each other's faults and forgive anyone who offends you. Remember the Lord forgave you, so you must forgive others" (Col. 3:13, NLT). Does it move your heart? What an exhortation. Personalize these commands and read them aloud.

Here is another *as*, this time in the Lord's Prayer: "Forgive us our debts *as* we also have forgiven our debtors" (Matt. 6:12, emphasis added). Dear friend, does this command put any urgency into your heart?

List all aspects of God's forgiveness for you. Review the characteristics of forgiving love: "Love…is not irritable, it keeps no record of being wronged…never gives up…endures through every circumstance" (1 Cor. 13:4–7, NLT).

Your forgiveness of another individual should have those same elements! God's forgiveness is complete, no holds barred. Your offense will not be remembered and will not be held against you. He gives you a clean slate. After setting that example, He commands: "Do likewise."

Now examine your relationships with others for any unfinished business in the area of clearing offenses. Ask God's Spirit to shed His light, bringing conviction as He did with the psalmist: "Search me, oh God and know my heart; test me and know my anxious thoughts, see if there is any offensive way in me, and lead me in the way everlasting" (Ps. 139:23–24).

What does the psalmist mean by "offensive ways" in you?

Dear friend, the Holy Spirit is working in answer to your prayer. Could it be *you* who needs to acknowledge that you caused an offense? Could it be *you* who needs to ask for forgiveness?

What role does confessing and grieving over *our* wrongdoing play in asking another individual for forgiveness?

Are you struggling with a particular offense or injury against you? What does erasing offenses mean?

Should it be a condition that others need to confess and repent *before* we forgive them? Or are we accountable to God to be obedient and forgive as an expression of godly love regardless? Refer back to the Matthew 18 passage. If necessary, also check Romans 12:18. Is there any excuse for extended grudges, coldness, and brokenness in relationships without taking steps toward understanding, forgiveness, and reconciliation?

Why is forgiveness so vital to the health of relationships?

Examine Matthew 18:15–17. What does God expect from us if fellow believers wrong us and conflict exists in the relationship? Are you responsible to seek understanding, clarification of their actions, and a resolution to the conflict? Why?

Dear friend, remember this: Our God is a God of relationships! He wants our relationships to be free from conflict and the resulting negative feelings and actions. It is vital for us to seek, understand, and extend forgiveness. He models those same dynamics in our relationship with Him. Remember that forgiving others does not mean we condone their actions or relieve them of the consequences. It means letting go of our resentment, anger, hurt, and desire for vengeance. Immediately stopping any recurring thoughts about the offense should be a consistent mental discipline. Replacing those thoughts with thanksgiving to God for His forgiveness ultimately brings freedom from recurring grudges that replay in our minds.

Furthermore, it means releasing that individual to God and giving up our "right" to see repentance and receive a plea for forgiveness. I have seen those dynamics work powerfully in the relationship with my mom. My family and I were blessed by her goodness countless times. Sadly, she also battled her little demons and often inflicted deep pain in my heart. In the process, the Lord taught me about forgiveness and ultimately allowed me to pray a salvation prayer with her when she was in her eighties. How blessed I was to know she went home to Jesus at age ninety-nine after we had shared her precious final years in closeness. The more thankful we are for God's forgiveness toward us, the easier it is to extend forgiving love to others. Forgiving others will always include the following steps:

1. **Seek understanding of the offense against you**. Most important, pray for the person who wronged you.
2. **Confess and lay down festering anger, judgment, lack of forgiveness, and hurt before God.** I like to visualize placing those feelings in a package, wrapping and sealing them, and putting them in the hands of Christ or on His shoulders on the cross, fully committed to leaving them there. At the same time, I need to release my right to be understood and to receive an apology, commit any judgment to God, and rest in that commitment (Is. 33:22).
3. **Forgive others who wronged you and, if possible, verbalize your forgiveness.** Release them to God's Spirit and His work in them, and do not hold the offense against them or bring it up anymore. This forgiveness also involves your decision not to allow the offense to linger in your thoughts or heart or to influence your actions. These are the greatest challenges, because your heart can be hardened, and your mind can be bent on rehearsing the offense.

4. Allow others to retain their sense of worth and dignity and support efforts toward their restoration if possible. **Continue to pray for them**.

5. If possible, seek communication to gain mutual understanding. Retain a humble spirit. **Choose to try to make things right.** God's Spirit will guide you and give you the right words. You may say something like this: "I care about our relationship. Can we talk and try to make things right?" You might not get the response you hoped for, but you were obedient and made an effort toward understanding and restoration. You begin to feel the burden and sadness lift. Maybe you have the response you hoped for and deserve, maybe not. There might be tears or disappointment. Keep praying for the individual.

6. **While you cannot control the outcome, you are walking toward freedom**. Remember the Max Lucado quote at the beginning of this chapter: "Relationships don't thrive because the guilty are punished, but because the innocent are merciful" (Max Lucado, Facebook post, February 11, 2013).

II. Principles at Work

The "As" Principle

> Forgive others as God has forgiven you as an
> expression of your love and obedience to God
> (Eph. 4:32, Col. 3:13, and Matt. 6:12).

The "Choice" Principle

Forgiving and erasing offenses is a choice, not a feeling. It is a decision, often not a desire. It is a command, often just as difficult to obey as loving the unlovable or the undeserving. It is an act of the will, and like all acts of obedience, it is blessed by our Heavenly Father and brings His rewards. Remember that in any wrongdoing against us, it is our interpretation of the offense that affects us most. Think of a careless, unkind comment a loved one makes. For some, it could be just that: a careless comment, easily passed over. For others, it could cause deep wounds, because they conclude that the individual does not care for them, and therefore the comment is intentionally cruel. With this perception of the wrong, forgiveness becomes that much harder. Once again, let us remember the difference between perception and reality: "Life is about 10 percent of what happens to me and possibly as much as 90 percent of how I read it."

> Here are some important questions to ask yourself: Did I read this wrong? Did I overreact? Are there confessions, adjustments, or compromises that I can make or suggest?
> Can you share a time when God blessed you as a result of your obedience in forgiving another individual?

How was your relationship with that individual affected? Did it help you to evaluate **why you hurt,** or **why the wrong** toward you **was done**? Were you able to demonstrate some understanding, realizing where the other individual was coming from?

Was the experience a faith builder?

Behavioral psychologists point out that in a large percentage of our relationships, we can just choose and determine to get along in spite of challenging interactions. That approach seems to describe people who **choose to communicate and compromise.** They choose to work through hurt and difficulties and therefore reach a point of understanding and some degree of resolution of the conflict. How does this look? You seek communication in an effort to understand, being ready to extend some grace. This decision toward conflict resolution necessitates a mutual willingness and often a clear statement of determination to give the relationship another chance. This choice is in keeping with your **commitment to the relationship.** Reconciliation in our human relationships does not necessarily mean that the initial quality of the relationship is restored, but we have made an effort to exchange thoughts and feelings. Both parties seek to gain understanding and a workable solution that is mutually acceptable. This search involves a **decision to try to get along.** Paul urges us in Romans, "Seek to live at peace with everyone" (Rom. 12:18). Instead, we often go from being bruised within to having a broken relationship, without seeking a mutual understanding and rebuilding. Thus, isolation and loneliness become marks of our society.

Sometimes there is a simple solution: Just to "let it go" for the sake of the relationship. Have you ever heard these wise words: "Let go and let God"? Have you not also realized that, with time, feelings tend to lessen in intensity? Beware of impulsive reactions. **Whatever course of action you choose, at the heart of dealing with offenses should always a gracious spirit.**

What is the counsel from Proverbs 19:11?

Richard Carlson wrote a small booklet called *Don't Sweat the Small Stuff.* He says that we too often waste emotional and relational energy and court negativity because we focus on small things. How much wiser it is to just overlook someone else's poor choices.

How does 2 Corinthians 5:17–18 address this issue? What does God call you to do? What honorable title does He give you?

We are ministers of reconciliation, a holy task that is very close to God's heart. Our efforts may go through several stages toward reconciliation. Sometimes the other individual will not respond as we had hoped. In those cases, the status of the relationship might not change, but we have been obedient, and this effort increases our inner peace. However, quite often, our relationship becomes more honoring to God, more meaningful and fulfilling than it has ever been before.

Often wounds and pain linger on. It might be necessary to set new boundaries that involve adjustments and compromises for the sake of keeping the relationship viable and helping it to survive. I remember the words of a wise friend after the unfaithfulness of her husband: "I choose to keep standing in the storm, but I adjust my sails." This decision to stay in the relationship and try to make it work has nothing to do with being in love and sometimes little to do with loving that person. It is a matter of intentional conciliatory actions to save the relationship by expressing godly love in obedience to our Heavenly Father.

Certainly, my friend, weathering the relational storms in our lives is always challenging and often discouraging. But without fail, using God's ways leaves us stronger, more committed, and more able to love as God loves. It was a joy to see the words of our daughter-in-law on Facebook on her anniversary: "I am not perfect and he [her husband] is not perfect. But we are perfect for each other." I know many compromises and much understanding were part of that resolution. It seems to me that she has the right idea.

III. The Principle of Freedom

The Word of God states, "Whatever you bind on earth will be bound in heaven and whatever you loose on earth will be loosed in heaven" (Matt. 16:19, 18:18). Binding is the opposite of erasing offenses.

This is a difficult and often misunderstood scripture. Applied to God's children, I believe it means the following: If we loosen others from the burden of guilt and the bondage of the offense against us by extending forgiveness and erasing those offenses from the slate of their lives, God's Spirit is loosened to bring them conviction and, hopefully, confession and restoration. This belief puts quite a bit of responsibility on us as we deal with offenses. Trust God's Word, dear friend. I find this principle to work powerfully in my own relationships. **Think of the awesome responsibility God gives you: to loosen His Spirit to go to work in someone's life.**

It is said that when we forgive and erase offenses, a prisoner is set free. We readily think the prisoner is the one we have forgiven, only to find out that it is us. Lack of forgiveness, resentment, anger, plotting revenge, being hurt, and feeling victimized are natural reactions to being wronged. These feelings and actions hold us hostage and can become our torturers (Matt. 18:34). In addition, by entertaining these destructive, negative feelings, we give continued influence over our lives to the one who caused the offense. This influence binds us to that individual, and we certainly don't want that! When we "let go and let God," we find amazing freedom and release. We are the prisoners set free.

How does Hebrews 12:1–2 address this issue? **Dear fellow sojourner in Christ, keep running that race, unhindered and not entangled, fixing your eyes on Jesus, the author and finisher of our faith, because of the joy set before you and the freedom found in Him along the path.**

IV. Application

1. What current relationship in your life needs to be reconciled?

2. Which steps do you plan to take?

3. Which burdens caused by wrongs done against you do you need to throw off?

3. Each day this week, pray Psalm 139:23–24. Begin by writing both verses on a little card that you look at several times each day. Listen to God for His answer and record it. Then follow His instructions.

   Dear friend, I pray these insights from God's Word put you on a conscious freedom walk. Thank God for setting you on that journey.

CHAPTER 8

Find Value in Each Person

"It is difficult to make man miserable if he feels worthy of himself and kindred to the great God who made him" (Lincoln and Bachelder 1965, 8).

FINDING VALUE IN ANOTHER INDIVIDUAL and feeling valued as a person are key elements in our relationships. This aspect of love helps foster genuine appreciation and honor in the way we perceive ourselves and others. Its absence fosters insecurities with knee-jerk reactions, coldness, and even aggression. It becomes difficult to set healthy boundaries in our relationships. People who do not feel valued come across as insecure or needy people. Unhealthy expectations on their part invite disappointments and hurt, leading to physical, emotional, and mental withdrawal. Tragically, the result is the sheer inability to form healthy relationships, leading to the destruction of mental, emotional, and physical health.

I. GOD GIVES US VALUE IN OUR RELATIONSHIP WITH HIM

Friend, you agree that being valued is one of our greatest needs. It helps determine our identity and sense of worth—or lack of it. In the chapter "Desire and Do the Best for Others," we laid a solid scriptural foundation for who we are in Christ and our new identity as children of God. **It is God who gives us value in our relationship with Him**. Listen to more of what

He says about us: He created us in His image, in His likeness, so we are His image bearers (Gen. 1:26).

What does this idea mean to you? *We* are His workmanship, His masterpiece, created to do good works (Eph. 2:10). He called us into a loving relationship, and we are His. He created us for His glory (John 3:16; Is. 43:1, 7).

How specifically does God express His love for you in those verses? Try to look into His heart and see what He feels, then make a note of it.

He made us a part of the family of God (John 1:12). We are His children, brothers and sisters of Christ. Just think: He chose us to be in a relationship with Him. He, the all-knowing, all-present, and all-powerful God, the Creator and Sustainer of the universe, made you a part of His family. We are His offspring (Acts 17:28). Do you feel honored, important, and valued? His presence with us is constant. Hear His promise from Zephaniah 3:17: "The Lord your God is with you, He is mighty to save. He will take great delight in you, He will quiet you with His love, He will rejoice over you with singing."

Here is the Lord of Lords and King of Kings who not only loves and values you but also desires your company, delights in you, and rejoices over you. Does that warm your heart and make you feel special? Can you even believe it, my friend? I memorize verses like the one above, and when times of heaviness or self-doubt weigh on me, I repeat those verses over and over until my spirit begins to lift. Put the following scriptures into your own words:

Colossians 2:9–12

John 15:15

1 Corinthians 6:19–20

Ephesians 1:18–20

Hebrews 13:5

Look at John 17. What does His high-priestly prayer express about the closeness and eternal security of our relationship with God? Find the many ways Christ values and cares for you. Do you feel safe and secure with Him? Write a note of thanksgiving.

My husband and I watched a *60 Minutes* segment of Lady Gaga with thousands of fans, hands lifted toward her, receiving eagerly what she offered. Beyond the grotesque appearance, she articulated a message later in an interview: "We can all be superstars." A spectator explained, "It helps me to believe in myself."

Recognizing our desire for validation, I wonder why is it so hard to receive Christ's message that we are sons and daughters of our Creator God, His friends, and image bearers of our Heavenly Father. **Why is it so difficult for God's children to feel validated and lifted up in these truths?**

God makes countless clear statements about who we are in our relationship with Him and His Son, Jesus Christ. Dear friend, I urge you, read, memorize, and meditate on those statements, until you are established, rooted, and anchored in them (Col. 2:6–7). This is our Lord's new software for our mind! That same passage in Colossians also tells us that living in such love leaves us strengthened and built up. Don't walk with your head down. Ignore and disregard the old identity programming! The almighty God values you. Abe Lincoln once said: "It is difficult to make man miserable when he feels worthy of himself and kindred to the great God who made him" (Lincoln and Bachelder 1965, 8). **The more we draw our strength from Him and accept His definition of us, the less we will be fooled by those around who claim to have life's answers.**

Because we are anchored in the truths of who we are in Christ, His Spirit guides us toward aligning our life choices with our value and identity in Him. With our hearts at rest, we can express thankfulness and praise to our Heavenly Father. That is His favorite way of receiving our love. It delights God's heart and lifts our spirit. It is our praises that usher us quickly into His presence, for He inhabits the praises of His people. And when we praise Him, we join myriads of angels in worship.

II. Find and Give Value to Other People

> "When we carry honor in our hearts for others, our value grows in their eyes, and we gain a place of influence with them" (Vallotton and Johnson 2006, 125).

Some time ago, I asked my son-in-law, a successful businessman, father of three teenage sons, and Christian mentor, what he considers the most important element in his interactions with other people. His response came quickly: **"Giving and communicating value to other people."**

Within every human being there is a God-given drive to achieve something and become someone of value. If we tap into that drive in others and demonstrate that we believe in all of their untapped potential, they will do almost anything to live up to our expectations. In the musical *My Fair Lady*, Eliza Doolittle, a common flower girl, becomes an elegant lady who mixes with England's society. How did it happen? Because Henry Higgins, the eminent linguistics professor, treated her like a lady, she began to live up to his expectations and the image he created of her in her own mind. This kind of visualization helps create a new reality for us—first in our thoughts, then in our feelings, and ultimately in our persona and actions.

These same dynamics are at work in our marriage relationships. Years ago, I remember the admonition of a pastor leading a marriage seminar: "Treat your husband like a king, and he will come to treat you like a queen."

There are many different ways to find and give value to others. Jesus modeled them for us in various encounters with people who were considered second-class citizens and outcasts in that society. Think, for example, of the woman caught in adultery in John 8. Jesus looked at her with compassion and said, "Neither do I condemn you, go now and leave your life of sin." He valued her as one created in God's image, and his compassion and grace turned her life around, right into the loving arms of God. We can't help but believe that she, lifted, redeemed, and empowered, spent the rest of her days trying to live up to Christ's view of her and, with a thankful heart, praising his name for her new life.

How did Christ validate Martha in John 11:17–27?

Describe the life-changing encounter between Jesus and the woman at the well in John 4:1–30.

The following tools of communication are effective in showing others their value to you: Cultivate positive thoughts and appreciation of them in your heart. Abe Lincoln reminds us that if we look for the good in a person, we will find it. Eye contact stimulates the brain's social-network circuits, decreasing stress hormones and increasing feelings of sympathy. Begin with words that convey genuine appreciation, realizing that the first words set the tone for the whole conversation. Be positive and affirming if possible. A sincere compliment can create trust. Establish common ground to help provide mutual understanding. Be careful how you close a conversation. The last words tend to linger on.

Giving value to others involves assuring them that they are not trapped in their present circumstances. We extend hope for change and build confidence toward the future. For example, share this promise by the Lord: "For I know the plans I have for you, says the Lord. They are plans for good and not for evil; they give you a future and a hope. In those days when you pray, I will listen. You will find me when you seek me, if you look for me in earnest" (Jer. 29:11–13, TLB).

Try to see others with God's eyes and validate their potential. The command to encourage and build each other up is woven throughout the New Testament. Sadly, criticism and judgment come to us much more easily. Affirming love will help others move beyond a struggling self-image and resulting poor performance, for love hopes all things and believes all things. We build up their confidence and hope by laying a new foundation of God's truth under their lives. It becomes the anchor of their new identity, encouraging acceptance of and faith in God's value assessment of them.

Your wish for their transformation will, hopefully, foster their desire to reprogram their minds by meditation on and memorization of these truths. I can see the joy and growing excitement as their new sense of identity becomes more of a reality. A chain of blessings has begun, to be continued in an outflow of these same truths to others. **It will flow in**

reassurance, affirmation, and appreciation expressed through words, actions, and attitude. In our own small sphere of influence, we began a chain of blessings that can lift and change lives. When we love as God loves, we love with His heart. When we love with His heart, we see people as He sees them.

Put the following scriptures into your own words:

Romans 12: 9–16. Specifically focus on the words "Honor one another above yourselves" (10b).

Ephesians 4:29

When we honor other individuals, we give value to them. When we find and give value, we build each other up with words of appreciation and affirmation. The famous Oklahoman Will Rogers stated, "I have never met a man or woman I did not like." He liked others because he purposed to find something of value in them.

Again remember, we are created in God's image. Although sin warped that image, there is still something of value in each individual. My grandmother carried these truths in her heart, purposing to find something good in every individual she met and found, in turn, favor in their eyes.

III. APPLICATION

1. Think of the fact that God wants to use you as His instrument of hope and transformation. Ask Him to show you someone who has been disheartened by circumstances and needs to be lifted up by feeling valued.

2. Create a special occasion to show how you value a friend or spouse.

3. Ask the Lord to help you to cultivate feelings of admiration and appreciation and to express them more readily.

4. What are the different creative ways you like to express value to another person? Which responses do you notice? Which ways seem more effective?

CHAPTER 9

Find Value in Adversity and Challenges

§

I. From Victimized to Victorious

Do you feel victimized by adverse circumstances? Do you wonder if God has abandoned you or turned against you? As result, do you question His goodness or favor toward you? Or do you feel just plain unlucky?

Have you ever looked for the silver lining in the clouds? Are you open to look beyond the difficulty of the moment to find some good, something of value, even in bad and difficult circumstances? **It is our Heavenly Father who brings value to our difficult times. He wants to show us more of Himself and increase our growth, trust, and faith in Him.**

> "God is painting a picture of grace on the canvas of your life. God is writing His- story, history with a hyphen, through your life. God is crafting your character through the circumstances of your life. To see yourself as anything other than God's masterpiece is to devalue and distort your true indentity. And it's in discovering your true identity that your true destiny is revealed" (Mark Batterson, 2011, 10).

The key is to see the situation with God's eyes. In the Chinese language, the symbol for *crisis* is a combination of *danger* and *opportunity*. Therefore, every crisis can become an opportunity, depending on how we deal with it. Simply put, what we experience as a crisis is an **opportunity for God to show His love, His grace, His provision, His guidance, and His power on our behalf.** Our difficulties are an opportunity for Him to show us who He wants to be in this specific situation and what He wants us to become if we depend on Him. His Word affirms to us that He wants to be our rescuer, our comfort, our guide, a strong tower we can run to, our shelter and safe place. Look to Psalms for passages that will encourage you in thee truths.

Faith and the right attitude will determine how we cope. No stronger words have I heard than those of the apostle Paul: "What is more, I consider everything a loss compared to the surpassing greatness of knowing Jesus, my Lord, for whose sake I have lost all things. I consider them rubbish, that I may gain Christ" (Phil. 3:8). **Clearly, our adverse circumstances and struggling relationships offer the greater value of gaining Christ and growing in our faith in and dependence on Him.**

Joseph, as portrayed in the Old Testament, was betrayed by his own brothers. After being sold into slavery, he ended up in pharaoh's court as second-in-command. He was then able to provide for all of Egypt and his family during a famine in Israel. He teaches us another value: see God's goodness and sovereign purpose being fulfilled in even the most difficult of circumstances. Giving a summary of all of his trials, he said to his brothers, "You intended to harm me, but God intended it for good, to accomplish what is now being done, the saving of many lives" (Gen. 50:19, 22).

He used a powerful tool for responding correctly to adverse circumstances. He reframed the events. Instead of feeling victimized by his brothers' ill intentions against him, he saw them as God's tools to fulfill God's perfect purpose in his life, namely, to save his family from starvation, having been made second-in-command over the food storehouses in Egypt.

What often hurts us most is not the offense against us (in this case, Joseph's brothers' jealousy and cruel actions against him), but our interpretations of the wrong done to us. Instead of focusing on their evil actions, Joseph saw God's goodness at work, not only on his behalf but also for the good of his heartless brothers and the whole nation.

Put Romans 8:28 into your own words.

God will use our circumstances, good or bad, to accomplish His perfect will for us. Does this help you, my friend, to find value in your present struggles? I can tell you that most of my growing as a child of God was done in difficult circumstances and while working through challenging relationships. God allows these challenges to happen in our own families, with a close neighbor, or in our daily work environment to accomplish His perfect, preordained purpose for us. These "irregular people" become God's sandpaper to soften our hearts, to teach us to learn to adapt and make compromises, and to increase our capacity to love.

Read and write out 2 Peter 1:5–8. Ponder the progression of how godly character is formed in us.

During my periods of struggle, I needed time with my Lord more than ever, and His presence was sweeter and more comforting than at any other time. He validated the practical working out of His truths, which at times conflicted with my human understanding. Those times of difficulty and testing have become my testimony. My "mess" became my message. Does that not put value in your difficult situation or struggle as well?

Job also understood the heart of God. He correctly modeled what our response to trials should be. Though deeply troubled and dismayed, he ultimately saw value in his tragic circumstances. He recognized that in the process of stripping most of his earthly blessings away, God was showing him more of God Himself. He stated with conviction that in the end, he will come forth as gold (Job 23:10–12). **He grew in humble acceptance and ultimately gained more of God Himself.** What important point does Job make in the following statements?

> "My ears had heard of you, but now my eyes
> have seen you, therefore I despise myself and
> repent in dust and ashes" (Job 42:5–6).

Look at Job 19:25–27. Do you agree with the statements in Job 1:21–22 and Job 2:10? Explain your answer.

How can we gain a deeper understanding of who God is? What is more important than coming to greater acceptance of His sovereignty and awesome power in all of creation and His mighty hand of love and goodness in our lives, even in times of struggling and challenging relationships and circumstances? **Because of our faith and trust in God, He works all things for good to those who love Him** (Rom. 8:28). He helps us to sustain hope, forge optimism, and keep a positive focus. He helps us rise above the circumstances with more confidence instead of being weighed down and pushed toward hopelessness. We can't be reminded often enough that Satan uses any struggles to take us down and cause our defeat. It is our choice to focus on the positive and move on in the hope that God will use even our adverse circumstances for His good purposes in our lives.

Write out Philippians 4:8–9.

Don't ever underestimate the power of positive, faith-based thinking. It is absolutely therapeutic. If adverse circumstances can teach us the merit of a hopeful, God-centered, optimistic mind-set, we can be counted among the winners in life.

Any negative thoughts or attitudes will take us in the wrong direction—doubt, bitterness, and stress. Reruns of a wrong endured or fears of stress ahead will only point you in one direction: down. That is where Satan hopes to take you. Therefore, do not allow yourself to dwell on any negatives, even for a moment: "For God has NOT given us a spirit of timidity, but a spirit of power and of love and of self-discipline" (2 Tim. 1:7). Other translations talk about a spirit of fear given us by Satan versus a sound mind given us by God. What is not from God, our loving Father, is from Satan, our adversary.

Now read Philippians 4:11–13. What did Paul learn?

During the days in which we struggle with discouragement in difficult circumstances, God wants us to cultivate a spirit of gratitude living out of our spiritual inheritance, the riches of His care for us, His children. When discontent and grumbling rise up in your soul, praise Him instead for His caring heart and the assurance of His goodness. This praise of God eases our burden, helps us find a different perspective, and delights God's heart. Over time, such a mental attitude benefits every part of our being and leads to easier acceptance of adversity and to contentment. **Contentment is defined this way: realizing that God has already given us everything we need.**

This is a small sampling of reasons to find value in difficult circumstances and relationships. God uses every challenge or crisis as an opportunity to do His good work of making and molding us into the image of His Son and build our inner strength and dependence on Him.

This is a very important point, dear friend! Mistakenly we think that circumstances or the right people define the quality of our lives. Instead, it is how we *interpret* those circumstances and respond to them. In partnership with God, believing in His continued love and goodness toward us, we see the "irregular" people as His sandpaper for the molding and making of our character. Difficult stretches of life help us become better people instead of bitter people. We move ahead as overcomers instead of feeling victimized. We build larger hearts, a stronger faith, and join the throng of God's children who face the future with confidence and hope instead of becoming discouraged and isolated in their pain or facing the wreckage of broken relationships.

> **Always remember, we cannot control or change our past, but in partnership with God, we take hold of the present and have an active part in shaping our future.**

When we find value in all of life's circumstances, our perceptions, attitudes, and outlook change. Romans 8:28 is validated: God will ultimately use everything for our good if we are genuine believers. We trust Him. We know that even though we might not see all the desired changes and solutions in our lifetime, God's goodness is still at work. We stand with confidence, anchored in His love, knowing He is fulfilling His perfect purpose for our lives. Such a faith fills us with hope and anticipation of how God will help us resolve the issues we are dealing with and strengthens us with confidence in our future. Just see and anticipate what good God will ultimately accomplish in partnership with you (Eph. 3:20). Give Him a chance to show His power and goodness to you, and recognize that in all things He is sovereign.

With acceptance of the good or bad in our lives comes another benefit. We avoid a lot of stress. **Stress has been defined as resisting what God brings to or allows in our lives.** Recognizing that we have a loving and sovereign God, very present even in our wilderness experiences, brings acceptance of our life situations and a confident dependence on His help and direction in navigating through them.

* What is the assurance you get from Hebrews 13:5–6?

Thus we come to say with confidence: "The Lord is my helper. I will not be afraid. What can people do to me?" Dear friend, do you see all the faith builders? Thank God for them! God wants to use everything that He allows to happen in your life to fulfill His perfect will and purpose for you. Here is what God speaks into the lives of His children: " 'I will not remove the scars from your life. Instead I will rearrange them in such a way that they have the appearance of carving on a fine piece of crystal.' Such is the love of God. What was despised becomes a testimony of God's grace—a thing of beauty" (Vallotton and Johnson 2006, 55). God has the same message for each one of us. **Your mess is your ministry, your test becomes your testimony, bringing honor and glory to His name and bearing witness to His love and power.**

II. The Lifeline of Prayer

All that the Lord wants to teach and show us as we navigate through adverse circumstances and challenging relationships is accomplished only with a life of prayer and full dependence on Him. This is our source of power and perseverance. From here springs our sense of God's loving presence with us, the confidence of being heard, the assurance of being guided, the hope of healing in our relationships, and the confidence to face tomorrow.

Prayer warriors are birthed in war. During times of intimate communion with our God, we are infused with confidence for the battle. Time spent in God's presence is the life breath for the child of God and the sustaining power when the going gets rough. Prayer has been described as putting ourselves into God and God putting Himself in us. It gives us strength, light, and direction for each day.

Prayer connects us to others and builds a community of faith. It compels us to look outward to draw in and touch others with the heart of God. Praying for people is vital for loving and seeing them with God's eyes and as God's instruments. It is foundational to expressing each aspect of love we've talked about. It is God's tool for melting hurts, anger, mistrust, revenge, hardness, and disappointment and for infusing His love and hope in us, while restoring peace to our inner world. It is our lifeline, our spiritual mainstay, and our foundation for navigating through any kind of trial. Prayer is the Holy Spirit's instrument for sustaining and molding us by using challenging and difficult circumstances to bring us to maturity in Him. It is through prayer that God forges a deeper and more sustaining faith each time we overcome adverse circumstances.

What does God command in each of the following passages?

Philippians 4:6–7

Romans 12:12

Matthew 5:44

Matthew 11:28

James 5:16

Matthew 21:22

Prayer and communion with God are vital to generate and preserve an intimate, empowering love relationship with God and to maintain that relationship as a priority in our lives. They are our source of hope and confidence when we face an uncertain future. It is because of sustained prayer that we prevail over temptations and resist Satan. In prayer we find guidance at the crossroads of life and are sustained in suffering by Jesus (Matt. 11:28–30).

"Prayer is the bridge between my unconscious and conscious life. Prayer connects my mind with my heart, my will with my passion, my brain with my belly. Prayer is the way to let the life-giving spirit of God penetrate all the corners of my being. **Prayer is the divine instrument of my wholeness, unity and inner peace**" (Nouwen and Greer 1999, 35).

"To pray is to unite ourselves with Jesus and lift up the whole world through him to God in a cry for forgiveness, reconciliation, healing and mercy. To pray therefore is to connect whatever human pain or struggle we encounter—whether starvation, torture, displacement of people or any form of physical or mental anguish—with the gentle and humble heart of Jesus. Prayer is leading every sorrow to the source of healing; it is letting the warmth of Jesus' love melt the cold anger of resentment; it is opening a space where joy replaces sadness, mercy supplants indifference, love displaces fear, gentleness and care overcome hatred and indifference. But most of all, prayer is to come and remain part of Jesus' mission to draw all people to the intimacy of God's love" (Nouwen and Greer, 1999, 36).

This is my prayer for you, dear friend: "May the God of hope fill you with all joy and peace as you trust in Him, so that you may overflow with hope by the power of the Holy Spirit" (Rom. 15:13).

III. Application

1. Think of a difficult situation in your life. What value can you find in it? How can God use those circumstances for His purposes on your behalf?

2. How can we avoid stress? What is the difference between being stressed and being distressed? Which of the two is definitely harmful?

3. Why is it so difficult to keep our thoughts in positive territory?

4. What are you willing to change about your prayer life? Where does it fit into your daily life?

5. Share a story about a special moment with God in prayer. Why is this moment significant to you?

CHAPTER 10

Give Grace and Show
Undeserved Goodness

〄

I. GOD EXTENDS HIS GRACE TO US

> "For out of His fullness (abundance) we have
> all received one grace after another and spiri-
> tual blessings upon spiritual blessings and even
> favor upon favor and gift upon gift" (John 1:16,
> AMP).

DEAR FRIEND, ARE YOU OVERWHELMED by God's goodness as I am? The good news is we are not living under the law, as Old Testament believers did, but under grace. Hear what Paul says: "For if, by the trespass of the one man (Adam), death reigned through that one man, how much more will those who receive God's abundant provision of grace and of the gift of righteousness, reign in life, through the one man, Jesus Christ" (Rom. 5:17).

Expressed more simply, this message is clearer and absolutely stunning: **All who receive God's abundant grace and are freely put right with Him will rule in life.** "Each of us who received Jesus as Lord of our life is to govern in the realm of life. All who have freely received God's grace are empowered to be preeminent over any adversity this world can throw against them. Life on this earth is not to rule us; we are to rule in life. Through the power of God's grace we are to change our societies just as Jesus did His. This is our mandate" (Bevedere 2011, 45).

This is a very powerful statement. Spend some time in your group discussing practical ways to obey that mandate. What are your thoughts about it?

There is more about grace in the word of God:

* Our relationship with God is anchored in grace (Eph. 2:8).
* He draws us by His grace (Acts 18:27).
* We are justified by His grace (Rom. 3:24).
* We grow and mature in His grace (1 Cor. 15:10).
* His grace empowers us and is sufficient for us to handle all things (2 Cor. 12:9).
* By grace He gives us eternal hope and strength (2 Thess. 2:16).
* His Word to us is called the *gospel of grace* (Acts 20:24).
* God is the God of all grace (1 Pet. 5:10).
* Christ embodies both grace and truth (John 1:17).

Grace is the essence of God's heart and being. How beautifully the old gospel song by John Newton, the former slave trader, expresses these truths:
Amazing grace, how sweet the sound that saved a wretch like me,
I once was lost but now I am found, was blind but now I see.
T'was grace that taught my heart to fear and grace my fears relieved;
How precious did that grace appear, the hour I first believed.
Through many dangers, toils and snares I have already come.
'Tis grace that brought me safe thus far, and grace will lead me home.
When we've been here ten thousand years, bright shining as the sun,
We've no less days to sing God's praise, than when we first begun.
It is God's grace that lets us see His goodness in trying situations. It is His grace that sheds His light into the dark places of our lives. It is God's grace that lets us consciously experience His presence and love. It is by His grace that our wounds are healed. It is by His grace that His mercies are new every morning (Lam. 3:22, 23).

It is grace that allows us to experience the blessedness and freedom of being forgiven. Personalize Psalm 32:15.

Without God's grace, our inner being is like a dried-up, thirsty sponge. To be saturated in God's grace, we must soak it up in times of prayer, worship, and heart intimacy with Him.

How did the psalmist express this idea in Psalm 42:1?

How many times each day have we been encouraged when overcome by our sense of weakness! Share God's promise in Paul's words in 2 Corinthians 12:9.

Do you agree with Paul's conclusion? Express it in your own words.

Think of a time when God's grace proved sufficient for you to deal with or endure a difficult situation. Write out your thoughts. Do you want to share it with the group for their encouragement?

Grace is God's answer to sin. It disarms Satan and renders him powerless. Sin does not surprise God. His faithfulness to us overrules sin. Forgiveness and restoration are the expressions of His love that draw us back. Grace continues to believe in us and boasts about our journey of becoming more and more like Jesus (2 Cor. 3:18).

Put Romans 5:20–21 into your own words.

Praise God: Where sin abounds, grace increases all the more. Grace brought us into a relationship with God and sustains that relationship when we fall away. Restoration is

God's tool of grace to bring us back to Him. His ardent desire is to restore us to the complete fellowship with Him that sin broke. His intention is to lead us on toward maturity and to fulfill His perfect purpose for us. He indeed wants to finish the good work He began (Phil. 1:6). **When we are anchored in grace, we experience again and again that our God is a God of restoration and second chances.** Indeed His mercies and compassions are new every morning (Lam. 3:22–23). Hear the psalmist crying out in faith and trust in God's restorative love: "Restore to me the joy of your salvation and grant me a willing spirit to sustain me" (Ps. 51:12).

Do you remember how Peter denied knowing Christ three times in the final hours of Jesus's life? A repentant heart and simple declaration of his love for the Master put him back on the path to restoration and ministry. "Feed my sheep" was the endorsement and command of His Lord, Jesus Christ, after his fall. This is grace.

1 John 1:9 holds true every time we come with a repentant heart to God. Confession affirms our forgiveness, brings cleansing for the soul and a restored fellowship with God, and renews the right spirit within us. God gives us a new start and wipes the slate of our conscience clean. We walk in freedom and power again. **This is grace.**

One of the best examples of restoring grace is found in the account of the prodigal son. Read the account in Luke 15:11–32. Describe the expressions of the loving grace that you see in the father's heart.

My favorite verse in this account is verse 20: "But while he was still a *long* way off, the father *saw* him. He was filled with *compassion* for him, *ran* to his son, *threw* his arms around him, and *kissed* him" (emphasis added). **He was lost, but now he is found.**

The son's role and standing in the family and his fortune were restored. Because of grace, he never lost his place in his father's heart, and the father was anxiously waiting for his return. When he came to his senses, grace welcomed him back into the fold. This is a powerful, heartwarming picture of how our Heavenly Father deals with us!

Grace is not a license to commit sin, but a humble acknowledgment that we have been given another chance. Each one of us experiences manifold expressions of God's grace in our daily lives. Sometimes we call them blessings, but most of the time we hardly notice. May we never take our moment-by-moment blessings, God's expressions of gracious love, for granted.

My dear friend, pause for a moment to go to a quiet place and commune with your Heavenly Father. Thank Him for the many aspects of grace at work in your life. This is a form of worship and adoration He treasures. Ask Him to open your eyes to the many expressions of his gracious love that so easily go unnoticed.

II. Extend Grace to Others and Participate in the Restoration Process

God counts on His children to become instruments and tools of His grace in the lives of others. We should feel blessed to be used by Him in this way. We know in doing so we reflect His heart.

Dear friend, every expression of love is an expression of grace. We portray grace when we forgive or respond to unloving acts with kindness and patience. We extend grace every time we bring a ray of sunshine into someone's dark days. We demonstrate grace when we "let go and let God" or let grace clear any possible offense. We show grace when we focus on the majors and overlook the minors as we deal with offenses against us. We live with grace when we forgive, let bygones be bygones, and look confidently ahead to the future. We live out God's grace when we deal graciously with our fellow humans and even when we extend grace to ourselves.

Our Heavenly Father asks us to be His vessel to bring practical aspects of grace to an individual who needs to feel God's goodness to heal in an atmosphere of grace. God might also ask us to partner with Him in the restoration process of a struggling or fallen individual.

These are the times God calls us to even more fervently express our faith in His good work of change in a person's life. He will indeed finish the good work He has begun, and the individual will be restored to a path of righteousness. Often God asks us to go beyond encouraging words and a supportive attitude and calls for a deeper involvement in that individual's life to manifest His restorative love.

Of what situation God is speaking in Galatians 6:1?

When people are caught in sin, particularly in God's family, we have the responsibility to help restore such individuals to fellowship with God and to their place in God's family. In Galatians 6:1, the word *restore* has medical implications. It describes a physician resetting a broken limb. Without that treatment, the person can only hobble along and will likely lose the use of that limb. That idea expresses the possible danger of fallen individuals stumbling in their relationships with God or becoming isolated from the community of faith, as might happen if people have to carry alone the burden of wrong, guilt, and rebuke from fellow Christians. Can you hear the cry from Job's heart: "A despairing man should have the devotion of his friends even though he forsakes the fellowship of the Almighty" (Job 6:14).

Living under condemnation and isolation is a cruel fate. Unfortunately, it happens far too often. This sad evaluation from the outside world seems to speak to that problem: Christians are the only army that shoots its wounded.

Understanding and acceptance of such individuals is needed here. We must have the ability to deal with the issue in a spirit of humility. Remember, we may not have committed their sin, but our wrongs are just as wicked in the eyes of God. Galatians 6:1 reminds us that temptation is just around the corner, and it is important to be on guard ourselves so that we will not be tempted (Galatians 6:1). Caution: pride comes before the fall. To help restore individuals spiritually we must prayerfully follow these steps:

1. Pray with them. Help them see and acknowledge their failure and sin. The prophet Nathan did that for David. Hear David's confession: "I have sinned and done evil in God's sight" (Ps. 51:4).

2. Guide them toward understanding and accepting responsibility for their sin. Even though someone else may have been a contributing factor, they are still accountable to God.

3. Counsel them on the basis of God's Word. Let them see God's heart of grace. Plead with God's Spirit to bring conviction and repentance. Repentance involves deep regret and sorrow over the sin committed, turning away from that sin, and moving in the opposite direction.

4. Lead them to accept and rest in God's love and forgiveness (1 John 1:9).

5. Help them seek restitution and make amends when possible.

6. Assure them of God's unchanging love for them and His intent and power to bring change and a better future. Build confidence and hope through your belief in them and the assurance that they will grow stronger and wiser through this experience.

7. Guide them in understanding that God teaches us through failure and will help them avoid similar mistakes as they lean on Him.

8. Celebrate a new beginning. Stay involved with prayer, encouragement, and accountability. Follow up! Help them to continue to walk in grace and hope.

In all issues of failure, sin, and the resulting guilt, it is important to understand the difference between repentance and remorse. Peter, resting and even confident of God's grace, portrays repentance after his denial: a godly sorrow of heart to have grieved someone he loves and regret over actions that were wrong and that God calls sin. Repentance is anchored in understanding God's heart of grace. It involves hope and assurance of forgiveness and restoration.

Judas, who did not know the heart of God, struggled with remorse after betraying Christ. This is Satan's intended course of action: ungodly sorrow without assurance or hope of forgiveness and restoration. It leads to despair and, in this case, suicide.

When God extends grace and asks us to be part of the restoration process, we must act in a spirit of gentleness. In Psalm 45:2, the psalmist talks about lips anointed with grace. More than likely, the individual we are dealing with is already hurting and fragile. Condemnation will only worsen that person's plight.

Put the following passages into your own words:

* Colossians 4:6

* Ephesians 4:15

Loving confrontation is facilitated by two things: a caring, loving relationship that gives us the "opportunity and right" to confront and a gentle, loving manner in the confrontation. This method of approach flows from a direct assignment from God, who wants to use us in the confrontation-and-restoration process. **Confrontation must always be done with the goal of restoration, not condemnation.** It is important for us to remember that Christ embodied both grace and truth (John 1:17). That recollection means we are both forthright and truthful in a spirit of loving grace. Our actions and attitude express affirming and supportive love. Such ministry points forward and instills hope.

Give the essence of Philippians 3:12–14. What is the essential attitude that Paul describes here?

What does Galatians 6:2 mean in practical terms?

Bear one another's burdens and so fulfill the law of Christ. The word *burden* means "a heavy load." Bearing one another's burdens implies the willingness to walk with others, weep with them, and work with them until the burden has lifted and they are restored. Help them focus forward, assuring them that our God of grace is indeed a God of new beginnings and second chances, loving a restored sinner ever so passionately. If the hurting cannot find grace, hope, and healing in the family of God, where can they be found?

III. Application

1. What aspect of God's grace is most precious to you?

2. Which area of extending grace toward yourself do you need to work on?

3. Earnestly search your heart. Is there anyone in your circle of love that needs to be granted grace and to receive help in being restored? Ask God to help you see and love with His heart.

4. What specific steps can you take to help that individual turn around and walk toward restoration?

5. Which aspect of being a "burden bearer" seems most difficult to you?

Those individuals who pray for us and walk alongside us toward restoration after we have failed will assume a very prominent place in our lives. They are God's agents of grace. Their godly and practical expressions of love will never be forgotten. They are God's instruments and become true life givers of the kind of life that Christ promised, the overcoming life anchored in grace (1 John 5:4).

REMEMBER

Read, internalize, and obey His word. Our love relationship with God is His greatest gift to us. Preserving and cultivating the closeness and vitality of that relationship is the greatest gift and opportunity to bring good to the self and others.

In that vital, close relationship with our God, we become the best we can be, bringing glory to his name by living out his love. We carry out the great commission, sharing the Gospel and fulfilling the purpose and destiny that God has for us. We ourselves are the greatest gift we can make to God, to those we love, and to the world around us.

> **"For from Him and to Him and through Him are all things. To Him be the glory forever! Amen"** (Rom. 11:36). Receive the same truths quoted from another translation: "For everything comes from him and exists by his power and is intended for his glory. All glory to him forever. Amen" (Rom. 11:36 NLT).

A Symbol of a Restored and Healthy Relationship

HERE IS ANOTHER BENCH. THINK of it as a symbol of relationships. This one is lovingly maintained. The surroundings are well cared for, and an arch with roses exudes a sweet fragrance. There is a brick walkway so that the bench can be reached anytime in any weather, always welcoming and always inviting. There are comfortable cushions that promise relaxation and refreshment. This is a favorite place where my husband and I have moments of refreshment and joy. It is a safe place, a place of rest, for heart-to-heart talks that build and sustain our relationship. As we sit and chat, we are blessed with special times of shared intimacy. These moments bring us closer and deepen our mutual understanding while we gain strength and joy from our time together.

What you see is just another bench, really—just a symbol. **The difference between the first picture and this one is an illustration of the difference that "loving as God loves" will bring to your life.** That difference in the quality of your life and your relationships will be monumental—yes, totally life-changing! There will be healing, new joy, amazing strength, and God's purpose fulfilled in your relationships.

Now, dear friend, go back to the first bench and continue reading! We are going to share an exciting, life-changing, and spiritual journey.

BIBLIOGRAPHY

Amplified. 2010. Grand Rapids, MI: Zondervan.

Batterson, Mark. 2011. *Soulprint: Discovering Your Divine Destiny.* Colorado Springs, CO: Multnomah.

Bevedere, John, 2011. *Relentless: The Power You Need to Never Give Up.* Colorado Springs, CO: Waterbrook.

Carlson, Richard. 1997. *Don't Sweat the Small Stuff.* New York: Hyperion.

Lincoln, Abraham, and Louise Bachelder. 1965. *Abraham Lincoln: Wisdom and Wit.* Mount Vernon, NY: Peter Pauper.

Facebook, Inc. "Max Lucado's Facebook Page."

Max Lucado, February 11, 2013. www.facebook.com/Max Lucado/posts.

NIV. 2007. London: Hodder & Stoughton.

Nouwen, Henri J. M., and Wendy Wilson Greer. 1999. *The Only Necessary Thing: Living a Prayerful Life.* New York: Crossroad.

Vallotton, Kris, and Bill Johnson. 2006. *The Supernatural Ways of Royalty.* Shippensburg, PA: Destiny Image.

Made in the USA
San Bernardino, CA
08 April 2016